Cryptic Crossword

Book 18

Edited by Richard Browne

Published in 2014 by Times Books

HarperCollins*Publishers*
77–85 Fulham Palace Road
London W6 8JB

www.harpercollins.co.uk

10 9 8 7 6 5 4 3 2 1

© Times Newspapers Limited 2014

The Times is a registered trademark of Times Newspapers Ltd

Richard Browne asserts the moral right to be identified as the editor of this work

A catalogue record for this book is available from the British Library

ISBN 978-0-00-751782-4

Typeset by Susie Bell, www.f-12.co.uk
Printed and bound in Great Britain by Clays Ltd, St Ives plc

INTRODUCTION

The puzzles in this book are selected from those that appeared in *The Times* during 2010, and are a representative selection of the work of our then 17-strong regular team. One puzzle (number 71) appeared only online, in the special Christmas Day edition. Two puzzles this year represent the final offerings of their compilers: number 8 is by Roy Dean, who decided to retire; and number 40 is by Mike Laws, former editor of *The Times* crossword, who died in 2011. We do not often print themed puzzles, but I put one in (number 19) to celebrate the seventieth birthday of choirmaster Martin Neary, under whom I sang for several happy years in Winchester.

As usual the final puzzles in the book are the complete set of Championship puzzles: four qualifiers and the nine puzzles used at Cheltenham on finals day. The three Grand Final puzzles proved particularly difficult, and only six of the 24 competitors completed them correctly in the hour allowed; the winner, once more Mark Goodlifffe, astonishingly finished them in a total of 24 minutes, by my watch a good 13 minutes ahead of the runner-up, Peter Brooksbank. In case anyone feels disheartened, I suggest looking at the rather more relaxed performances of the competitors in the preliminary rounds, and remembering that nowadays we only allow 20 minutes per puzzle, against the half-hour that was standard twenty years ago.

For anyone new to our crossword, we start our collection with a sample puzzle for which the workings of the clues are all explained in detail. The solutions to all the other puzzles are of course at the back of the book.

Richard Browne
January 2014

A BEGINNER'S GUIDE TO *The Times* CROSSWORD

ACROSS

1 Soldiers in country, kind mostly set for dramatic work providing lessons (8,4)
8 Dancer turning against study course (7)
9 King with focus outside court? That's nonsense (7)
11 Bone that's ending in stew (7)
12 Knock received by most of retiring drummer's equipment (7)
13 Assistant for one wanting a good round container (5)
14 Unorthodox messenger endlessly carrying quote around (9)
16 One with cold at home surrounded by rubbish used medicinally (9)
19 Gnomes in Icelandic tales (5)
21 With regard to work, nothing in month succeeded (7)
23 Retain ground next to motorway for tower (7)
24 Worried after term back in spring (7)
25 Resentment from dogsbody giving up resistance and working (7)
26 Mushroom created by prof, then, only after explosion? (4,2,6)

DOWN

1 Just weary, capsized in sea (7)
2 Utterly unknown, ring up, interrupting meeting (7)
3 Through time, hard to stop efficient monster (9)
4 Volunteers go off in pack (5)
5 Drop prize paid (7)
6 Article on artist with aim, excited about language (7)
7 Turbulent priest at once examining body (12)
10 Black stream? An element in that is oil (12)
15 Space used in printing poem in list, for example (4,5)
17 Much ridicule over hotchpotch (7)
18 Better spot yielding opening for leader (7)
19 Expected row about new city (7)
20 Saloon? Jolly place to dine (7)
22 Bank needing husband to enter identity (5)

NOTES

This detailed explanation of the cluing methods for this puzzle should show you plenty of techniques (for example, some abbreviations) that are used in most of the other crosswords. I have indicated the definition elements in bold type: you will notice that virtually every clue has both a definition and a cryptic element (so these two routes to the answer should enable you to crosscheck your answer and be confident it is correct); and that the definition always comes either at the start or the end of the clue (useful tip!). Never be seduced by the surface meaning of the clue; it is designed to deceive. Look at the individual words one by one, and see what function they serve in the build-up of the answer.

5

ACROSS

1 Soldiers (OR – other ranks) in country (MALI), kind mostly (TYPE minus its last letter) set (LAY) for **dramatic work providing lessons** (8,4) = MORALITY PLAY

8 **Dancer** turning (reversal indicator) against (V) study (EYE) course (RUN) (7) = NUREYEV

9 King (R – Rex) with focus (HUB) outside court (BAR, *which can mean a particular court of law*)? That's **nonsense** (7) = RHUBARB

11 **Bone** that's ending (T – the ending of "that"!) in stew (PAELLA) (7) = PATELLA

12 Knock (PAN; both words mean *criticise*) received by (ie inside) most of retiring (TIMID minus its last letter) **drummer's equipment** (7) = TIMPANI

13 **Assistant for one wanting a good round/container** (two definitions) (5) = CADDY

14 **Unorthodox** messenger endlessly (HERALD minus last letter) carrying quote around (CITE, reversed) (9) = HERETICAL

16 One (I) with cold (C) at home (IN) surrounded by rubbish (OFFAL) **used medicinally** (9) = OFFICINAL

19 **Gnomes** in Icelandic tales (5) = DICTA (hidden in Icelan*dic ta*les)

21 **With regard to** work (OP, a musical number), nothing (O) in month (APR) succeeded (S) (7) = APROPOS (OP + O inside APR + S)

23 Retain ground (anagram of *retain*) next to motorway (M) for **tower** (7) = MINARET

24 Worried (ATE) after term back (NAME, reversed) in **spring** (7) = EMANATE

25 **Resentment** from dogsbody (DRUDGE) giving up resistance (minus R) and working (ON) (7) = DUDGEON

26 **Mushroom** created by prof, then, only after explosion? (anagram of *prof then only*) (4,2,6) = HORN OF PLENTY

Down

1 **Just** weary, capsized (TIRE, upside down) in sea (MED) (7) = MERITED

2 **Utterly** unknown (Y, a mathematical unknown), ring (O) up (reversed), interrupting meeting (RALLY) (7) = ROYALLY

3 Through (VIA) time (T), hard (H) to stop (go inside) efficient (LEAN) **monster** (9) = LEVIATHAN

4 Volunteers (TA, Territorial Army) go off (ROT) in **pack** (5) = TAROT

5 **Drop** prize (PLUM) paid (MET) (7) = PLUMMET

6 Article (A) on artist (RA) with aim, excited (AIM, anagram) about (C, circa) **language** (7) = ARAMAIC

7 Turbulent priest at once (anagram) **examining body** (12) = INSPECTORATE

10 Black (B) stream (RILL)? An (AN) element (TIN) in (inside) that is (IE) **oil** (12) = BRILLIANTINE

15 Space used in printing (EM) poem (ODE) in (inside) list (ROLL), for **example** (4,5) = ROLE MODEL. Notice the neat use of 'for example', which doesn't look like the definition.

17 Much (FAR) ridicule (RAG) over (O – cricket) **hotchpotch** (7) = FARRAGO

18 Better (CAP) spot yielding opening (STAIN minus its first letter) for **leader** (7) = CAPTAIN

19 Expected (DUE) row (DIN) about new (N) **city** (7) = DUNEDIN

20 Saloon (CAR)? Jolly (VERY) **place to dine** (7) = CARVERY

22 **Bank** needing husband (H) to enter identity (SELF) (5) = SHELF

THE PUZZLES

1

ACROSS

1 Kisser is person cut short, rebuffed (4)
3 I hope saint will convert Africans (10)
9 Comrade carrying revolutionary's weapon (7)
11 City demonstrates prominence, winning endlessly (7)
12 What recipient of message did that's said to be important (3-6)
13 Coalition, something painful putting British off? (5)
14 School in part of cathedral that's right for piano (12)
18 Those folk, old guys accommodated in military building temporarily (3,3,6)
21 Expect a majority in the auditorium (5)
22 Special chain deal for restaurant dish (9)
24 Part of engine that hasn't been scratched (7)
25 Make record of crushing snub (3,4)
26 Season for pantomime written by namby-pamby dramatist (4,6)
27 A bit of the rosary monk recited (4)

DOWN

1 Tree in flower, at the foot of which there's 'orse (8)
2 Country dweller in Nova Scotia at one time eating rook (8)
4 In the middle of battle there's little bird song (5)
5 One priest arranged to mediate (9)
6 Provider of a big bang? Possibly it's supersonic (13)
7 A woman absorbing English epic from the past (6)
8 Privileged young woman borrowed money maybe to be in the Home Counties (6)
10 Still being charged? (13)
15 Terrible quarrel that comes to an end at Hyde Park Corner (6,3)
16 The writer with opening poem, *Mound Builder* (8)
17 Last among spellers, having *taught* as *taut* (8)
19 Judge fraud, having caught out family member (6)
20 Rubbish bag initially dumped in side building? (6)
23 Head runs game (5)

2

ACROSS

1 Runner rejected speaker's gift, a child's toy (7)
5 Tense about performing song from *West Side Story* (7)
9 Hit the roof over expedition being private (11)
10 Half-hearted Indian ready once for literary gossip (3)
11 Old organ needed for stage show (6)
12 Governor's caught in a sleazy bar? That's sticky! (8)
14 Strippers' code designed to produce group loyalty (6,2,5)
17 Tiller in protégé's position, failing to impress (13)
21 Young person needs support introducing princess from East (8)
23 Self-confidence Sir Thomas displayed crossing a lake (6)
25 It provides shade by the Spanish motorway (3)
26 Fruit yours truly's nanny consumed by river (11)
27 Earnest European taking port in South America (7)
28 Soldier to continue following a way back (7)

DOWN

1 Keep stiff upper lip, going over US city? (6)
2 Get a group of singers to read aloud (7)
3 One who expects a sweetener from his workers? (3-6)
4 Sound way of walking, making entrance (4)
5 Rip-off connected with seat of Irish kings? Nonsense (10)
6 Poke first of girls with nothing on (5)
7 One may fix lights, being ultimately less industrious (7)
8 Note about partygoers makes us cross (8)
13 Quarter day claim has me rattled (10)
15 Officer at Aldershot initially eating cool sausage (9)
16 It may be flying as vessel turns up at lock (8)
18 Visionary description of an Oxford spire? (7)
19 Youth leader leaves country with business for wool producer (7)
20 A woman's age is required, supported by this (6)
22 On which one may examine an expert without pressure (5)
24 Characters from Tredegar climbing well over the hill (4)

2

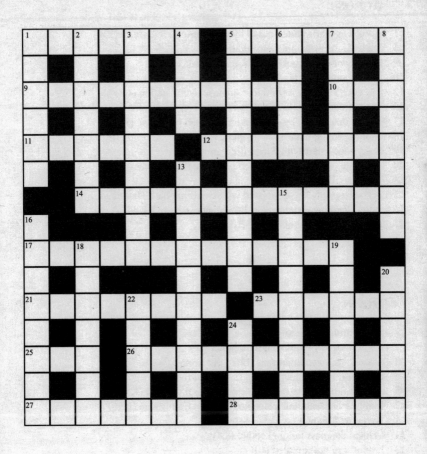

3

ACROSS

1 Amplifier that's reliable used by decision-making group (10)
6 Smart clubs welcome Conservative (4)
9 Mouth-watering cooking oil's in a vat (10)
10 Ravel's sandpiper (4)
12 Murdoch's putting an end to biometric identification (4,8)
15 Scripture lesson by cleric after epistle from Harris, for example (9)
17 Smoke discovered by one beginning to get in vehicle (5)
18 Quite attentive to personal hygiene (5)
19 Spicy food's extra in US city (9)
20 As a rule, gives change for deli purchase (5,7)
24 Wine pavilion (4)
25 Is Harris primarily associated with chaps in boat? That may be fine (10)
26 What's lacking ultimately in Providence, Rhode Island (4)
27 Source we will get out of jail (10)

DOWN

1 Say nothing about Anglo-Saxon band (4)
2 It's not fair to describe duckling thus (4)
3 Distracting form in journal (12)
4 Conspirator in middle of road confirmed rising (5)
5 A contralto forced to take time out for oral passage (4,5)
7 Looking for academic place not far from Cambridge (10)
8 Agree with Stoic to review classes (10)
11 Critical business talk in brothel (8,4)
13 Explorer in hut revealed (10)
14 As a rule, cover beans in mess (10)
16 Amber fluid guaranteed opening (9)
21 Not going anywhere yet (5)
22 Fairy in danger? Not entirely (4)
23 Male toiletries initially filling sink (4)

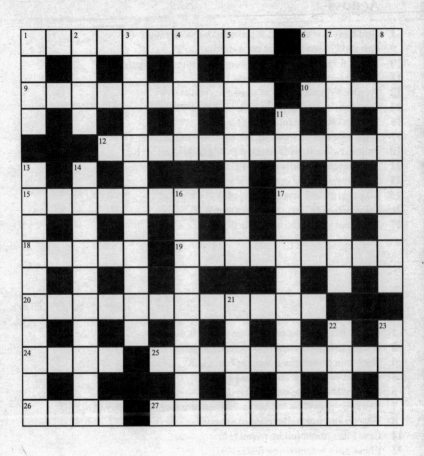

4

ACROSS

1 Golf club in which food is provided between rounds (8)
9 Part of US seen by many on stage (8)
10 Mate's turned back, skirting constant danger to shipping (6)
11 Reinforced, yet reversed course (10)
12 Prepare to publish part of screed I typed (4)
13 Napoleon's shopkeeper at home in castle (10)
16 Term in Oxbridge college (7)
17 With time moved forward, sell art that's outstanding (7)
20 Political system, as is covered by Marx, primarily (10)
22 Text secretary finally put on PC (4)
23 Laid down the law in cricket side I criticised (10)
25 Like carrier lost at sea, perhaps (6)
26 Spice mixed by servants, for example (8)
27 Her yacht was at sea, as a rule (8)

DOWN

2 Part of letter from a person who posted it, say (8)
3 Boxing title, oddly, initially defended against amateurs (10)
4 Not being present for a term of Latin (2,8)
5 Prisoner of ancient army a long time (7)
6 Flap endlessly, like wings (4)
7 It may be played — but not in live performance, apparently (6)
8 Pilgrim and storyteller cooked salmon outside (8)
14 Cow I had, sheltered by friend (10)
15 Cheer pilot for repairing this? (10)
16 Like a sensitive soul, so to speak, hard to handle (8)
18 Border on driveway (8)
19 Take temperature inside and it's unusually cold (7)
21 One with home in Hundred Acre Wood, something difficult to rent (6)
24 Writer whose sister had one? (4)

5

ACROSS

1 Start to choose a dog, say, to keep in the city (4,4)
5 Medicine once a school subject, briefly (6)
10 From measure of energy usage, black mark put down? (6,9)
11 Concerned with black poet turning less interesting (7)
12 Side in green, during a long period? No, blue (7)
13 To assault a contemptible man is instinctive (4-4)
15 Look sound — one on the way up (5)
18 Fatal day, behind hospital screens (5)
20 Generous husband? Even more than that (8)
23 One's puffed up with the wind, and suffers earache? (7)
25 Very small creature decapitated on motorway (7)
26 Give order to us, yet for certain we can do what we like (3,1,4,7)
27 Good amateur, but he makes lots of pairs (6)
28 Issue anorak when it turns mostly cold on the front (8)

DOWN

1 In China oddly cold these days for one that loves the heat (6)
2 Was material recovered from pirate den? (9)
3 Pains that follow witches' toil? (7)
4 In fight stabbed with iron, this thin? (5)
6 Left in terrible shape at end of illness — that's unfortunate (7)
7 Wader is first to trip in layer of mud (5)
8 Songbird holds note — it may be hanging in the air (8)
9 Spies monarch shortly in fur (8)
14 King's Chapel not opening — signal to stop (8)
16 As a learner, am sent down, having wasted a term — here? (4,5)
17 Having babies' portion, but put weight on (8)
19 To grab is naff — leave a bit (7)
21 By agreement knocking off criminal is creating gratification (7)
22 With words, make puns and continue having fun (4,2)
24 Soldiers' flash device (5)
25 Sparkling stuff hard to find in one of a set of books (5)

6

ACROSS

1 Spotty student taking wheel encased in copper (6)
4 The tube strike one often had to lead (5,3)
10 Pops round tablet at a party twice and no more! (4,2,1,4)
11 Coat's short frilly collar turned back (3)
12 Actor's one in green room at the start (7)
14 Ape and bird — like the one in 10 (7)
15 One adversely resolving to enter home today? (5,2,3,4)
17 Graduate has affair with physicist in Oriental location for a change (7,7)
21 A Dublin broadcaster's short film on goddess (7)
22 King's mistress returning to court from Kashmir? (7)
23 Team doing tricks with ball are in red (3)
24 Pushing through bar, way inside (11)
26 I ask chef specially for this (8)
27 Nick has time for a run still (2,4)

DOWN

1 These throbbed, so rest somewhat reduced? (8)
2 Potential life sources spelling the end for many Russians (3)
3 Proclaim praiseworthy triumph over one fairly hollow (7)
5 Someone who's upset that fool is holding mug up (2,4,8)
6 Old, corrupt German's also pompous (7)
7 US showman Polish ace shot up badly (7,4)
8 One old king the other king upset (6)
9 Pushing through root and branch reform of new, or dark, tactics (6,3,5)
13 Being out on the loch, I caught Texan swimming (11)
16 Man books house round the corner — probably not for this! (3,5)
18 Poet's dwelling valuable, although unfinished (7)
19 Engine fluid from container outside toilet raised temperature (7)
20 Remote is waste of time without right button shape (3-3)
25 Top cake maker finally out of pudding ingredient (3)

ACROSS

1 Returned total amount in a spirit of hostility (6)
5 Secured a railway line between states (8)
9 Strong part of speech by Conservative edited (10)
10 Support side spectator can't see (4)
11 Old Roman piece is unread in translation (8)
12 Put on carpet that's old and torn (6)
13 What's central to proclamation for spiritual leader (4)
15 Precision cardinal initially brought into a church position (8)
18 Head towards game in Africa (8)
19 Said to plead for help as victim (4)
21 One in quartet producing church music (6)
23 With popular aromatic wine, I consumed starter (8)
25 Tempestuous author who was Irish, not English (4)
26 Rough judgment of visitor before one match (10)
27 City lost, in last resort accepting opponent (8)
28 Criticise sample in food store (6)

DOWN

2 Shark in harbour (5)
3 Indication of intelligence male agent mishandled (6,3)
4 Ass one put, under pressure, into equine facility (6)
5 Irritating advisors behind steering group (4-4,7)
6 Play too passive a role that's covered by legislation (8)
7 Fix computer problem resulting from awful budget cut (5)
8 Obscure European revolutionary repeatedly holding monarch after monarch (9)
14 Defender in a sport finally getting point (9)
16 People who fix faults in theatre flyers (9)
17 Clear difference between rivals that dawns on us (8)
20 Heavy cover that protects ring from the elements (3,3)
22 To help cut down work, erected platforms (5)
24 Teach new arrangement of Trout quintet (5)

ACROSS

1 End the term on being displaced (12)
9 Short of a little energy to turn page for youngster (5)
10 Heavy table to be employed by judges (9)
11 Popular tenors to be trained as lead singers (8)
12 Less considered type of food (6)
13 Bitterness found with one drug in pharmacy jar (8)
15 Make last English king start to exercise in the open (3,3)
17 Stop some of fungicides I started (6)
18 Old actress's grand farewell performance (8)
20 Withdraw from Bible classes with false piety (6)
21 Lily, a girl holding a job briefly (8)
24 Son set out remarkably smoothly, not letting up (9)
25 Vale with pine covered in gold (5)
26 Go mad, becoming sectioned (12)

DOWN

1 Wind god working for Air Chief Marshal (7)
2 Latest cars sent for repair — detective stepped down from vintage Bentley here (6,4,4)
3 See what gravestones often have (5)
4 Innovator's book going for a shilling in editorial office (8)
5 Spoils of war (4)
6 Statesman managed to suppress demand after peak (9)
7 Humanity student losing marks in play penned by literary collector (14)
8 Craving in the endless Irish way? (6)
14 At home, because engineers may be laying it on (9)
16 Where workers learn to get in drink to cure a cold (5,3)
17 Constraint with what's worn round university (6)
19 Good artist wins praise, going up in small steps (7)
22 One with a wizard personality (5)
23 A game uplifted by a distinctive character (4)

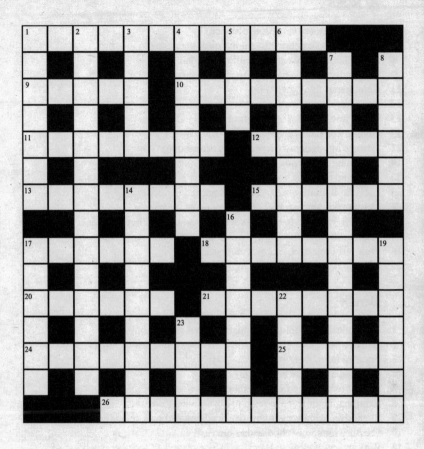

9

ACROSS

1 Pop round, run over greater distance (7)
5 Solicitor has something to eat in pub (6)
8 Control number of carriages allowed in halt (9)
9 Tongue I savour — but not the Spanish version (5)
11 Courageous flag-captain (5)
12 Real thugs can bring this about (9)
13 Graph transferred from chapter I (3,5)
15 Opposed to state's economics initially (6)
17 Closure imminent when pressure's dropped (6)
19 Draw near a very quiet fish (8)
22 Imagined wrong is avenged (9)
23 Dickens, with reason, died only once (5)
24 This part of Spanish bull pierced by tip of sword? (5)
25 Old university has to adapt, providing accommodation for people with higher degrees (4,5)
26 Fruit tart I rejected, and fish sent back (6)
27 Bit of maize revealed by my new horse (7)

DOWN

1 Temporarily abroad, lead is missing from show (3,3,7)
2 Book 8 (7)
3 Houdini in trouble (5)
4 Cover again checks on river (8)
5 Predict fish will be found in shop (6)
6 Examination of some quango in government (5-4)
7 Flier advertising very innovative academy that only recently opened (7)
10 Creature randomly chooses her bra (9,4)
14 With the cards dealt to them, do bridge players fit together easily? (5,4)
16 Record I had turned up in church — I'm seen everywhere (8)
18 Grieved horribly, becoming separate (7)
20 101-letter question — answer comes up as "connected with water" (7)
21 Startled Turkish commander's on time (6)
23 Object reserved but not finally suitable (5)

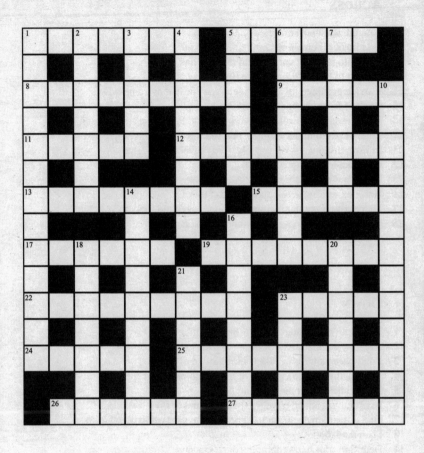

10

ACROSS

1 Tanned, showing sort of duskiness (3-6)
6 War favours certain wines (5)
9 Trying to repeat a sharp sound (5)
10 Prompt to redevelop giant site (9)
11 Provide evidence for magistrate about unusual awareness (7)
12 Profited from hearing a secret (7)
13 Sizeable savings available here in colony: face some struggles (7,2,5)
17 Parcel I put in luggage space, say, heading off on this? (7,7)
21 In love, disadvantage being old? That's worrying (7)
23 Oarsmen learned to swim (7)
25 Necessary to remain in place during most of Mass (9)
26 Hang something in the playground (5)
27 Diocese gets regular income from one good investment (5)
28 Girl in turn is to move slowly and almost fast (9)

DOWN

1 Lambs he's slaughtered here? (8)
2 Are they comparatively hard — to paint? (5)
3 From warm corner in valley, bird headed off (9)
4 Not healthy, swallowing last of meal with practised speed (7)
5 I'd flip stick, a rod for spinning (7)
6 Artist covers island in yoghurt and cucumber (5)
7 One working with string has go with line encased in metal (6,3)
8 Firm date (6)
14 Dear Salvador half-embraces courtesan (9)
15 Decline to visit icy fell (9)
16 Hotel has information identifying bomb-maker (8)
18 Showing amazement when ban is imposed over biassed presentation (7)
19 Horrid situation, even speaking Greek (7)
20 Millions root for socialist craftsman (6)
22 Waiting is all nasty? (2,3)
24 Physician needing to heal himself in practice? (5)

ACROSS

1 I'm thick-skinned, pressing Conservative with one hour to make a U-turn (10)
7 Whose artwork is vacant, lacking intensity? (4)
9 Notable decline involving glaciers etc retreating (8)
10 He wrote about robots almost synchronised with my gestures? (6)
11 Composer of a measure of music — tons, certainly (6)
13 Here it isn't out of place (is to be written out)! (8)
14 Like George Harrison, I land up playing on organ (12)
17 Such answers won't settle burning questions (12)
20 Primate listened to dull recording (5,3)
21 Prohibitionist's placard (6)
22 Indelibly write note as a cashless payment (2,4)
23 Some train GI snipers to go round military mark (8)
25 Child gaining weight set out to grow (4)
26 Apt accompaniment to queen of puddings is important for colony's future (5,5)

DOWN

2 What makes a man flustered? Latin (8)
3 Unfulfilled requirement to indicate old name (3)
4 Chain's first part of one confinement facility (5)
5 Kin were sympathetic (7)
6 Islam isn't disguised totalitarian ideology (9)
7 Mayor's wife reaching 100 mph? (11)
8 Giving coats to these islands' couples could make lazy work less (6)
12 Uneasy state, haphazardly partitioned (11)
15 Rosy narcissus having risen over viper (4,5)
16 Whale film casting unknown for ability to act without direction (4,4)
18 This useful service can be arranged any time (7)
19 Hollywood actor with husky parts to perform (6)
21 On top of lasagne, cut simple aromatic leaves (5)
24 My brain scan is inverted (3)

ACROSS

1   Aggro where British done, five arrested (6)
4   Braggarts having extra words to say among posh floozies (8)
9   Minute taken to steal ring? Yes! (7)
11   Newsworthy — time to move in for viewing (7)
12   Wake to find bird on end of duvet (5)
13   Extended as forks are to collect soil, odd bits escaping (9)
14   Always in operation obliged to follow hospital circular (10)
16   Fail to find maiden (4)
19   Silent movie cut (4)
20   Common, where there is extra meal laid out (10)
22   Mean somehow to keep neon in its natural state — an element (9)
23   No geek pens book in computer language (5)
25   Three consecutive notes let down (7)
26   Annoying to try karaoke after a drink (7)
27   Film about return of money for the unemployed composer (8)
28   Something to lose, given wide figure? (6)

DOWN

1   Fascinated to see comedian and revolutionary in the sack (9)
2   Character instrumental to *Twelfth Night*? (5)
3   Sprawl among scattered pears, viewing fruit tree forced flat (8)
5   Bond's beneath you perhaps, it's said (13)
6   One's beaten, being rubbish as well (6)
7   See English troubadour getting high, inhaling joint (9)
8   Reliable, then top (5)
10   Potential danger when open vessel is at sea, unknown number aboard (13)
15   Careless minister in mismanagement of fund starts to undermine leadership (9)
17   One shines, so shop is visible? (9)
18   Learned to accept measure as modern (5-3)
21   Useless ruse entering country, short of a hoax (6)
22   Lines taken through short distance, so connecting device (5)
24   Take first of boats over sound (5)

13

ACROSS

1 Approval for coercive measure (8)
6 Saint on Welsh peninsula denied right to die (2,4)
9 Hue associated with tint in print (4)
10 Reformed tart busy drawing? (10)
11 It had other fluid to go (3,3,4)
13 Intimate hugs just begun in time (4)
14 Song with single note occupying leaders in Oval Office (1,4,3)
16 Juniper not starting to turn green (6)
18 First person abroad with first lady's manservant (6)
20 What long leg is doing for novelist? (8)
22 Dolly, for example, runs 29 (4)
24 Unorthodox thinker not in command of mine output — until now (10)
26 Runaway serf felt so easy (10)
28 Cox and Co emulated cocks (4)
29 Container ship (6)
30 An artist only worked in carmine, vermilion, etc (8)

DOWN

2 Submit and get right away, using key instead (9)
3 Talk rent up for piece of property (7)
4 Silly introduction for nonsensical article that is put out (5)
5 Headcase for head (3)
6 Piano duet oddly entertaining British prince (5,4)
7 Heard greeting Big Brother? (7)
8 Like every second number after second number (5)
12 Discontinuous ruler available for less (2,5)
15 Scented plant making Holmes act strangely (9)
17 Quaker colonist ultimately wanting Quaker correspondent (9)
19 Virginia Water finally promises to pay divers (7)
21 Really fed up with shoddy coat (2,5)
23 Back from Glasgow — provided, that is, one's a Scottish woman (5)
25 Ratty needing river? Yes, initially (5)
27 Peter Rabbit's content to miss the mark (3)

ACROSS

1   Extreme party people: not a piece of cake remaining! (4,4)
5   Miss Piggy's outside reflecting in a low voice (6)
8   Green light put on wheels (3)
9   Adult female attending courses at school (6,4)
10 Loves lively, original, animated girlfriend (5,3)
11 A team's outside left skipping second half to see girl? (6)
12 Jam or Clash's Number One record (4)
14 Group supporting Charles I's chasing victory in board game (10)
17 Call in bar — sort providing non-alcoholic drink (10)
20 From the east, hail a Korean screen goddess (4)
23 Hall in university getting a tidy round (6)
24 Showed deference — or anything due — when following king (8)
25 English speaker holding a CD back gets one in a pickle (3,7)
26 Minister's brief to produce spin (3)
27 Touch filter in need of repair (6)
28 Come before tailless golden eagle, say (8)

DOWN

1   One used to carry fare: bacon rolls with mash (6,3)
2   Stick doctor next to old composer (7)
3   Spooner's partly abbreviated name for harmonica player (6)
4   A scream following weapon's appearance in madhouse (5,4)
5   In cracking bone, upset dish (7)
6   Jack in supporting post incurs penalty, maybe (5,4)
7   Elegant writer putting pen to paper for shopper? (7)
13 Barking dog won't, if found out (3,4,2)
15 Be ecstatic to have minor sort of part on show (4,2,3)
16 One not going to bed in suit is ultimately warmer without I see (4-5)
18 Ruling woman being inferior, not qualified to be Speaker (7)
19 Weird sorcerer producing rifle (7)
21 A pair lie without energy, being pessimistic (2,5)
22 Are there times when a tip goes round? (6)

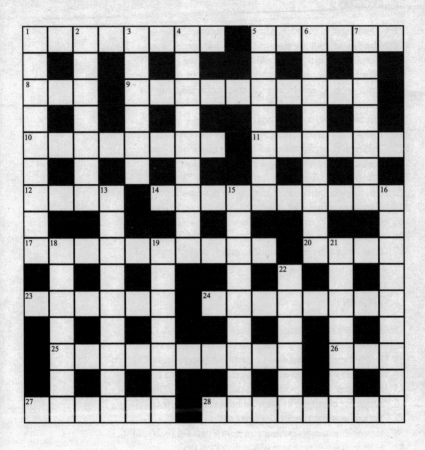

ACROSS

1 The height of classical Greek architecture? (9)
6 How to address woman in Mothers' Union? (5)
9 Buddhist writing about old lady in Eastern island (7)
10 Huntress in woods I met, rapidly retreating (7)
11 Little woman embracing the object of friendship (5)
12 Lack of activity, woefully on decline (9)
13 Oil etc found in region near Caspian Sea (5)
14 Crew arrange with king way to get on board (9)
17 Increase covering daily addition to cost (9)
18 Unstable fighter making many comebacks (5)
19 Abusing race, I'm the offender in this (4,5)
22 Champ who put one screaming on the canvas? (5)
24 Exercises a fine bird, one from Asia (7)
25 Combine parts of return journey in remote region (7)
26 Stark negative response of Scots to King Edward (5)
27 Creator of advertising whose work is highly regarded (9)

DOWN

1 Lost after temperature rises in one constituency (2,3)
2 What's left of article with, say, knot tied around it (9)
3 Badly typecast, husband is ready for minor roles (5,4)
4 Editorial work seen in theatrical anthology (7,8)
5 Many contenders, oddly, outside ring act formally (5,2,8)
6 Lead, for example, as director of agents and others (5)
7 Fellow holding me up, the fiend (5)
8 It provides many openings for ship's captain on island (6,3)
13 Silly emphasis on name being distorted (9)
15 Tsar crossing European border or boundary (9)
16 Taking unorthodox stance, and upwardly mobile (9)
20 Change direction in boat covering right course (5)
21 Rabble taking away ship and gold from this, for example (5)
23 Person on walkabout greeting king and queen (5)

ACROSS

1 Finally defeated, like Granny Smith examining mail? (6,2,3,4)
9 Aptness of the French leaders replacing clubs in survey (9)
10 Wood a female detective identified right away (5)
11 Live with son, discriminating against women? (6)
12 Security devices placed in front of lights (8)
13 Distiller's vessel making a comeback (6)
15 Quietly leaves drink one's oddly not selected (8)
18 Angels the writer's represented with English harps, perhaps (8)
19 Wearing rings, left for city (6)
21 Old PM's requirement rejected by sailor king (8)
23 Timid person consuming second dessert (6)
26 Synthetic product recent divorcee talked of (5)
27 Donkey that's amusing, or otherwise? (9)
28 Award one in Drake's ship's exchanged for a fish (6,9)

DOWN

1 One who studies Lima's head of state, perhaps? (7)
2 Bloomer made by church congregations, say (5)
3 Not appear to hear woman's concealing a deterioration (9)
4 Part of popular northern river (4)
5 Support article identifying problem in infancy (8)
6 Half of them satisfied a tourist in Cornwall (5)
7 Tyrant's papers in surprisingly poor binding (9)
8 Crime near to failing, going to arrest head of state? (7)
14 Wrong involving workers attached to the Italian plant (9)
16 Thick-skinned types welcoming creditor with a spiced wine (9)
17 Crotchety being going over his novel (8)
18 Reportedly contemplate pellet in gastropod mollusc (3,4)
20 Manage to upset vicar in old diocese (7)
22 Southern states long without possible cricket team (5)
24 One dividing charitable donations up in Indian city (5)
25 Article about drama soon to be written (4)

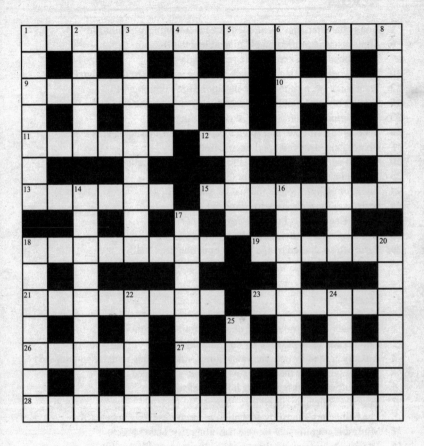

ACROSS

1 Leo's characteristics mentioned in a few meaningful words (4,6)
6 Stone circle identified by old man at length (4)
9 Don't be afraid to keep article secure (5,2)
10 Little woman coming in to pack, heading west to a holiday island (7)
12 Shelter not waterproof on the outside? That's ominous (10)
13 Feature of Eliza Doolittle's speech early on in drama (3)
15 Companion looks for people to run meetings (6)
16 Such as Marco Polo, first to visit east and return unexpectedly (8)
18 Bread, fizzy drink and pud ma ordered (8)
20 Church employee comments about cross being installed (6)
23 Lesson held by biology master (3)
24 Inside of eg Van Gogh's journal causing a stir (10)
26 Order, say, brought back to island (7)
27 Funky line in Elvis Presley's *Suspicion*? (7)
28 Heads of state in this European location (4)
29 Returned so shattered, and still in poor condition? (10)

DOWN

1 Club compère introduces top class entertainer's debut (4)
2 Famous dancer is pursued by fan, we may hear (7)
3 Anxiety caused by conscientious objector demanding to enter country (13)
4 Strauss symphony making a row — piano is drowned (6)
5 Court official working during holiday season (8)
7 Business colleague raised hire charge (7)
8 The belt is introduced by education authority as punishment (10)
11 Minimum requirement for one travelling first class? (4,3,6)
14 I will be below top in school tests — these are to blame (10)
17 Support for miners a long time after strike (8)
19 Fish cake, Yorkshire style (7)
21 Wild beast heartlessly seizes stray dog (7)
22 Ill-judged, finding employment round Camden Town area (6)
25 Old convict's first to be released from behind bars (4)

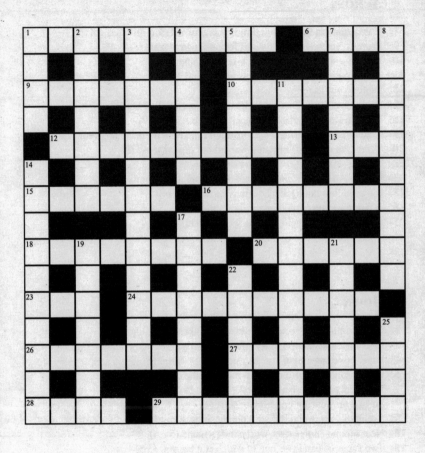

ACROSS

1 Contestants in this should pull in a big crowd (3-2-3)
9 Prevent one missing first signs for a very long time (8)
10 Having a shocking potential to be remembered (4)
11 A consequence of botched prison rescue (12)
13 Seafood's affected in South Island (6)
14 Son's cherished? That's not right, but superficially plausible (8)
15 Taxmen waiting at last for upper-class retaliation (7)
16 Ketch, perhaps hitting a steamship? This might describe the pilot (7)
20 North Sea region the French wanted back? Nonsense (8)
22 Turn to seize short-tailed domesticated fowl (6)
23 During Australian film, one old American is unpromising (12)
25 Ravaged, but not aged? This may be the cure (4)
26 What might turn out to mention a name (8)
27 Head of cattle showing a well-tended condition (8)

DOWN

2 One saddled with recurrent period of higher education? (8)
3 Beer mug aroma around the place regularly promoting passion (12)
4 Paper covering end of war in place of *The Times* (8)
5 Repeat Queen record needs to move up the chart (7)
6 Pea plant perhaps requires stick, planted in sheltered area (6)
7 Turned up wearing one minute skirt (4)
8 Svengali's art is playing with phony singer's head (8)
12 Neat second choice over wild panda's name (5,3,4)
15 Two types of panda — one of which is a big star (3,5)
17 Superfood? A doctor's sounding more optimistic (8)
18 Chaotic state results in humiliation for heads of British Library internally (8)
19 Want to be held by old nurse and relax (7)
21 No new programme dealing with organic fuel (6)
24 One without mark, the height of perfection (4)

ACROSS

1   I left alcoholic drink — I am a saint! (6)
4   Bird pulling back end of wing flying from here (7)
9   Good to avoid mountain tops in travels (5)
10 Slow change as popular uprising is headed off (9)
11 I am almost home, seriously! (2,7)
12 One speaking forgets lines — nicker results (5)
13 Take down spoken form of service (4)
14 For information, men grab computer industry founder (10)
18 Women's society does this, or fails (10)
20 Disadvantage of bomb development centre having mission taken away (4)
23 Cheap ticket, but initially restricted (5)
24 Operation determining the appearance of Macduff? (9)
25 Pay attention and note Hamlet stabbing king, in Shakespeare (4,2,3)
26 I agree to maintain a temperature that baker needs (5)
27 After many hours sailor sees the sun (7)
28 Member of religious society runs into the Devil (6)

DOWN

1   Male hanging around to enjoy festival (5,4)
2   Revolutionary assembly, we hear, is for no chicken (3,4)
3   Protect home? Of course (6)
4   Farm bird with missing foot (5)
5   Going out with reluctance at first in cold journey (8)
6   Deer fence thrown round river (7)
7   Singer's note has no vibrato in the middle (5)
8   What may make you a doctor? Look again! (8)
15 My attempt to secure honour in school subject (8)
16 Read notes carelessly, and struck a chord (9)
17 Zones included in domain name for region of world (4,4)
19 A number in disgusting housing, including flat (7)
21 We must support old woman (cow!) (7)
22 Advocate wife should be in bed (6)
23 Disposed of holding one had in firm (5)
24 Lift the mood of one in three, perhaps (5)

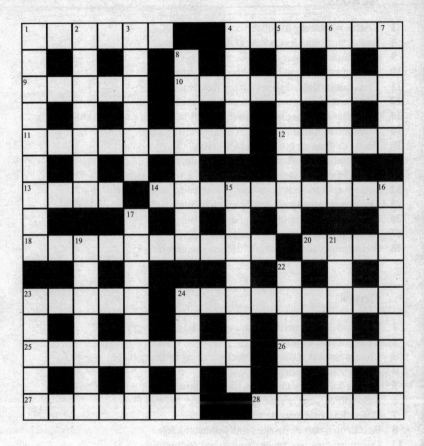

20

ACROSS

1 Briefly, something to entice you into books? (5)
4 End of story which is boring (5,4)
9 Check made by tutor during break (9)
10 Be seen going round lake on morning stroll (5)
11 Short period needed to secure the rope (6)
12 War memorial constructed on path behind church (8)
14 Supporter attending home match has left before the end — so childish (9)
16 Ambition to run saloon? (5)
17 Ready to drop, on coming in half-drunk? (5)
19 Downgrades opportunities for extra income (9)
21 Policeman I note stops lout committing act of violence (8)
22 Shortly arrived back at university, beginning to study, here? (6)
25 Matches invariably not beginning to light (5)
26 Finally putting sign up again for fruit (9)
27 Maybe football supporter's magazine (9)
28 Something made from fabric darners use regularly (5)

DOWN

1 Child covered in terrible bruises rants and starts to cry (6,4,5)
2 Group of riders thrown? (5)
3 Change needed at the top, if doctor's going to flourish (7)
4 Part of something insubstantial (4)
5 After a dry start in this place, day will turn stormy: get prepared (2,3,5)
6 Naval officer, one in marine environment? No way (3,4)
7 British Rail in a struggle to find lender (9)
8 Best known part of Brontë family drama (3,5,7)
13 Queen isn't put out, squeezing into box for premiere (5,5)
15 Lucky swimmer sheltering in safe place close to shore (9)
18 Money is raised, kept in store (7)
20 Erudite King Edward (7)
23 Record rising to top position (5)
24 Northern flower display (4)

ACROSS

1 A quality of sound doctor to work through fatigue (6)
4 Food in pub sent back by me, eaten by pussy (8)
10 Scratched and beaten outside room (9)
11 Cleric heading off to meet a woman (5)
12 He's had clash with tutor resolved after lively discussion (8,3)
14 Joke triumphed in the auditorium (3)
15 Chat and drink to establish close relationship (7)
17 Concentrate as some field is tilled (6)
19 Whence gold that is associated with scripture? (6)
21 Greek place allegedly very hot — vitality reduced by 50% (7)
23 In field, metal detector originally banned (3)
24 Sporty types having ball game at back of big 'ouse (3-8)
26 Wicket with slope offering turn (5)
27 More showy eastern garment (9)
29 Prepared to snatch the scrambled run when there's overthrow (8)
30 Conservative meets Soviet group to establish trust (6)

DOWN

1 Showing no end of sensitivity, I go quiet (8)
2 Estate requiring bloke in place of missing female (5)
3 Get about to collect duck eggs (3)
5 Communist club that may be growing in California (7)
6 Esau notably exceptional? Excess hair could be removed here! (6,5)
7 English firm has squandered monies — time to do this? (9)
8 Go to get composer after end of concert (6)
9 Customer's right laid down in court (6)
13 Senator well able to become filibusterer (11)
16 Bird in a park tree — cuckoo (9)
18 Film just out? Looks horribly revolutionary (8)
20 One outlaw follows army having left radical political group (7)
21 One of the pack heard this pipe (6)
22 American agent admitting regulation is wrong (6)
25 Like computer mail — half lost, the other half being set apart (5)
28 Music in standard keys always at the start (3)

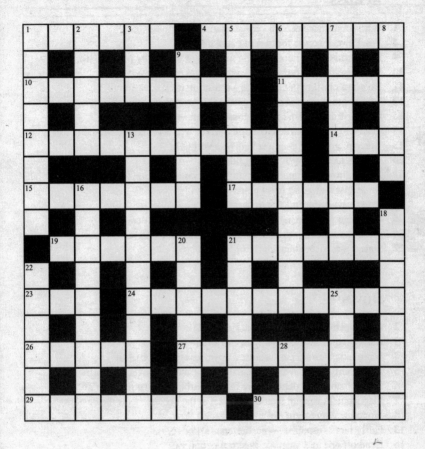

ACROSS

1 Where tea's not hot, and very strong? (4)
4 What's your recipe for making jam? (3-2-3-2)
9 Programme showing returning displays of temper by players (10)
10 Vehicles about to be supplied with special braking system (4)
11 No good wearing hat to create a sensation (6)
12 School governor and others offering support to chairman? (8)
14 Demonstrator doesn't have her spirit (4)
15 Maybe Scotsman article printed in error with two names misspelt (10)
17 Ancient Greek course in school? Capital (10)
20 Anorak rejected by 50% of children (4)
21 Mountain shelter intact after start of summer? Wrong (4,4)
23 Dramatist's singular misfortune (6)
24 Sign that's displayed at hen party? (4)
25 European political party's speaker who adds extra details? (10)
26 Make moderate proposals, in sad-sounding way (10)
27 Stainer's terrible sounds (4)

DOWN

2 Hard work using computer package? (11)
3 Dandy out of fashion, going to C&A for a hat (6,3)
4 Is almost penurious, as reported in yesterday's news (3-4)
5 In furthest part of America, earth tremor warning over California? (7,8)
6 Mass of sand was deposited in part of harbour, barring entry (7)
7 Flag some European countries raised at the borders, as is the custom (5)
8 Working class origin (5)
13 Fairly recent republic — earlier ones failed (6,5)
16 Head off ape and antelope in safari country (9)
18 See ecstasy being smuggled into disco raves, and more ecstasy later (7)
19 Business saved by one that's taken over my careful financial management (7)
21 Police raid succeeded: court proceedings just starting (5)
22 Old, awesome Athenian character (5)

ACROSS

1 Farsi song or poem's kept back in expectation of complaint (9)
6 Having nothing on end snake dance (5)
9 Constant backing for different networks (7)
10 Railing's causing injury (7)
11 Fastener to flourish when clipped (5)
12 Particular person, on reflection briefly, short and plump for a queen (9)
13 He died some distance from China, pierced by English daggers (5)
14 Nil-all and one-each replays: senseless repetition (9)
17 Turning back on immorality, a flash western Lothario (9)
18 Spoon-feed butter (5)
19 Bringing comfort with pound, as loan shark's cross for a second (9)
22 Oral promise: that would-be bride hopes to make it up! (5)
24 Abbreviated description of, say, Broadway's old tavern court (7)
25 Glass, china blocks joined between the edges (7)
26 Last of course to go out for the interval (5)
27 Having nothing on ends snake dance (9)

DOWN

1 Poser sinks bottom right in the dessert! (5)
2 Steer dogs past wide swamp (9)
3 Healthy one performing great number (9)
4 One cracking gags — or saying it's better not to? (7,2,6)
5 Boxers — one plucked hair, delivering unpleasant punishment (5,5,5)
6 Legal officer's bungle overlooking a fine, it arises (5)
7 Capital, singular, fur coats (5)
8 Sort of food almost everyone, surprisingly, eats these days (4-5)
13 Ranks novel about a poorly revolutionary, describing it? (9)
15 Muck in conclusion I'm surprised to find in ground (4,1,4)
16 Movement at grass-roots level a great electoral success (9)
20 Noble element love turning up to vote (5)
21 Rep leaves complaint, making member of family carp (5)
23 Likelihood team's opening pair have got out? (5)

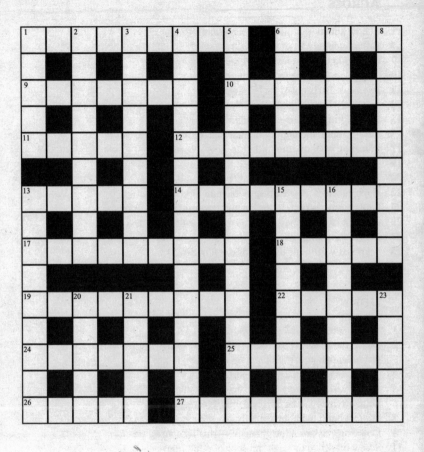

24

ACROSS

1 Fellow added to profit in second contest (6,5)
7 Bully opening can of worms (3)
9 One thing that's excessive (9)
10 There's an R in the month, stupid! (5)
11 People of Paris noted for hard work (7)
12 Tape rhapsody, in part? Possibly (7)
13 Bust of king artist initially submitted (5)
15 Group appearing nightly in Paddington, for example (4,5)
17 Sincere transformation of left to right of centre (9)
19 Fish about for material (5)
20 Huge insect found by mother (7)
22 Importance of article about nobleman (7)
24 One having no faith in Italian composer — up to a point (5)
25 As form of investment, it turns out badly, none the less (4,5)
27 Desire for change in East (3)
28 Frantically get appeal in for first offence (6,5)

DOWN

1 Strike force that was put on warship's bow (3)
2 Dance music is last part of broadcast on radio (5)
3 Fulminate about a politician, up in arms? (7)
4 Not having clue, oddly unimportant (9)
5 A long walk, parking vehicle first (5)
6 Some rhymes can be dull and uninteresting (7)
7 Interact badly with jury, finally producing conviction (9)
8 Don won't risk making changes — this'll secure a tie (7,4)
11 Screw that'll go through the door of one's house (4-4,3)
14 Bird getting head caught in main trap, possibly (9)
16 Full state of boy after consuming repeatedly at one (9)
18 Cream tea, say? Right — put on a little weight (7)
19 Soft cheese runs on one priest's garment (7)
21 Frequent search after article's hidden (5)
23 Take over illegal business, quietly replacing unknown, finally (5)
26 One of the lower digits compliantly put on line (3)

ACROSS

1 Taken for a ride, putting tool in carrier (6)
4 Free gift from old wife to poor sort of lady (5,3)
10 Scrum getting on with binding (9)
11 Norwegian's attention finally given to one problem on farm (5)
12 Listening device concealed by old counsel that's securely legal (3,4)
13 Find little fault with egg choice (7)
14 So much medicine, not at first for native American (5)
15 Sensitive type worried about Persian queen losing her tail (8)
18 Very pained, so gained extraordinarily? (8)
20 Crush a Muslim dignitary (5)
23 Playwright is engaging a single company (7)
25 Tell of decision after poll's close? (7)
26 With both hands, slide some piping, we hear (5)
27 Muse tried to translate part of Shakespeare (9)
28 Be stunned, as one may on beautiful night (3,5)
29 Quiet song that's followed religiously (6)

DOWN

1 Extremely excited: over the moon — new moon (8)
2 Row of shops shortly coming to one area in rural paradise (7)
3 Drink up, and beat a German — here? (2,7)
5 Gang activity is decreasing, or I'm crazy (9,5)
6 The meaning of snow? (5)
7 Idiot is interrupting extremely brilliant jazz player (7)
8 Working, drop round to fell tree (6)
9 Over a week, speculate this sensation won't endure (4,4,6)
16 One-legged challenge is hard work — put a stop to it (9)
17 Part of log needs singular stamina to cut up (8)
19 Teeing off to go round links, originally not one of those chosen (7)
21 More cheeky of one to enter alien craft (7)
22 Most beautiful American wife (6)
24 Show disgust about Left's disunity (5)

ACROSS

1 Drunk's chosen to imbibe litres (7)
5 From obese state see a change to current health (7)
9 Dismiss restaurant worker that drops one stiff drink (9)
10 Decibels I got from quad bike can make one shudder (5)
11 I shot rook in this tree (5)
12 Jogger needs to include a rest (9)
13 Reward prisoner with television channel allocation (13)
17 Like a gentle character we met — pestered, unfortunately (5-8)
21 Car flooring put together by functioning robot (9)
24 Scenery and dress mostly provided by men (5)
25 A house up north is grand with one toilet outside (5)
26 Using a needle gives sharp pain, including skin irritation (9)
27 Form of English that should be apparent at Dartmouth? (7)
28 Very serious promise (7)

DOWN

1 Bird with large beak having restricted breathing to a great extent (6)
2 Have distinctive feature in mind — an ornate scroll (9)
3 Base of hill of less than average height (3-4)
4 Decide to discourage working (9)
5 Meeting minutes in favour of university going ahead (5)
6 Drink a lot of something to keep you warm in a cuppa (7)
7 Antelope from Eastern province of Austria (5)
8 Son's leading in using bad language (8)
14 Talkative former partner criticises wives heartily (9)
15 Such reasoning invited upper-class Conservative's constituents to switch (9)
16 Convert a missile that's out of order (8)
18 To millions returning a high ball is fair game (7)
19 I get less of Casanova, perhaps showing resistance for seconds (7)
20 Bishop's morally good and intelligent (6)
22 Some matelots turned up for hire (2,3)
23 Quick to anger if not allowed to speak in court (5)

ACROSS

1 Rickety shelter for sheep extremely loose (10)
6 In Malay, a hard-working nursemaid (4)
8 Study language, inviting small number in for chat (8)
9 Monster goes mad, beginning to swim across river (6)
10 Wine Saint John, for one, left (4)
11 When all-round athlete may be seen, come what may (2,3,5)
12 Time when young boxers should start their training? (9)
14 Prize head of school received for sacred song (5)
17 Party thrown ultimately for Poe's bird? (5)
19 Work-book with test for examining pupils, etc (9)
22 Gaunt old American meeting fellow in saloon (10)
23 Being in the sea, it's regularly dissolved (4)
24 North American native given a bed in Mayfair (6)
25 Work-shy party taken in during period of abstinence (8)
26 Run over son in front of prison (4)
27 In alarm, decline European transport charge (10)

DOWN

1 Somehow prepare ideal cakes initially, using this? (4,5)
2 Rebuke motorway worker gets over illegal snare (7)
3 Firmly sealed composition that's difficult to obtain (8)
4 Remain inconspicuous like a flower Pope recollected (4,1,3,7)
5 Perhaps Adelaide needed half of them, investing £25 (6)
6 Self-seeker's stay I brought up in rare agitation (9)
7 Ways gunmen set up a weapon store (7)
13 Sort of paint Doré required to sustain a hobby? (9)
15 Plant-eater possibly let loose on root of vine (3,6)
16 Guardian gave space to footballing howler (5-3)
18 Language a wealthy husband dropped, having a degree in it (7)
20 Hardy character taking a long time to secure tile (7)
21 Fail to justify felon's first conviction (6)

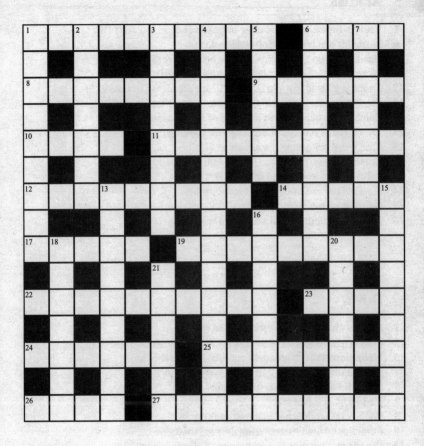

ACROSS

1   Vault over piece of wood close to gangway cracking craft (10)
6   Spade for one burying clubs and racket (4)
10 One lucky having fine physician as bookmaker (5)
11 Writer injecting element of great value into one murder novel (2,7)
12 Training ground gets old Premier League leader in trouble (9,5)
14 Something to do with pudding topping, say: last of icing (7)
15 Combustible heap almost in centre of old monument (7)
17 They'd cut a deal: it's in exchange for backing (3,4)
19 Card game my granny passes about (7)
20 Cross, by pony, path a nun travels (3,1,5,5)
23 Labour Party unlikely to split? (5,4)
24 Steal part of wall, taking odd sections (5)
25 One due a letter from Split (4)
26 Grocer's combining kicks and hard work (6,4)

DOWN

1   Put one's hands together for hit band (4)
2   Return fixture football team to play at last, no matter what (3,4,2)
3   Wells work daily, bottomless pit outside a church (3,4,7)
4   Spotted small flier being lifted by lawyer in drag (7)
5   It may be sucked down beneath cement (7)
7   Variety of rose bud (5)
8   Endless fat sandwiches in a row, soaking (10)
9   Prodigious drinker smothering duff in jam (6-2-6)
13 Wheels on firm ground ram bottom of plastic canopy (7,3)
16 Cold and coming down outside, most important to button it! (9)
18 Sort of protest rulers and numerous other leaders voice (7)
19 One making cold call, having zero information (7)
21 Writer Kipling denied ever meeting (5)
22 Report making little splash quietly cut (4)

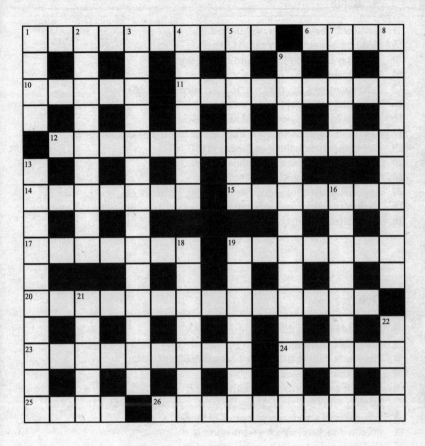

ACROSS

1 Get shot of welcoming resort in post (8)
5 Right backs without any caps (4,2)
9 Cricket ball split by Lancashire opener, say (3,5)
10 Trendy wine set (6)
12 Where men may be trained to jeer a conservative (7,6)
15 Cover close in game (5)
16 Broadcast of extremely trivial variety? (7,2)
17 Confusing my boot with his, like George in *The Famous Five*? (9)
19 Badminton competitor's qualification (5)
20 Western fan seeking an unusual book title (9,4)
22 One pound cut in tax? That's novel (6)
23 Approving of demo, oddly enough, during broadcast (8)
25 Neglect two girls, having borne son (6)
26 Inclination of general, say, about to lose power (8)

DOWN

1 Intended to put on thinking cap (10)
2 See rabbit, climbing, fall (3)
3 Previously willing to support a Labour leader (7)
4 Bats hit hard repeatedly (12)
6 Indian possibly shot in quiet university (7)
7 Stealing without a single thought — that's preposterous! (3,4,4)
8 When school's over, record a piece of music, too (4)
11 Press run rackets in such a tournament (6,6)
13 Urchins spoiling funfair games, short of energy (11)
14 Failing to give wife her stout (10)
18 Collection of writings found in vehicle (7)
19 Scrub computer key inside protective covering (7)
21 Finish off learning card game (4)
24 American concealing mounting fury (3)

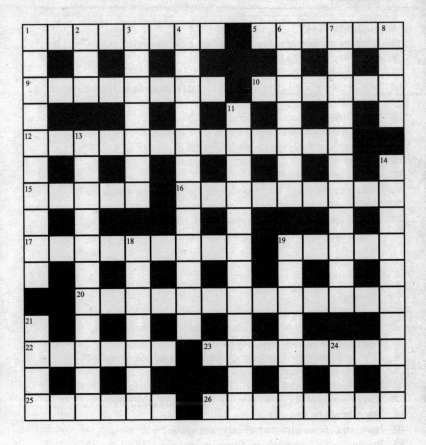

ACROSS

1 Leather mask (4)
3 Investigators having to keep on feeding a dog lover (10)
9 Light from the abyss? (7)
11 Terminal dedication from Heathcliff? (7)
12 Film character's evidence of hurt allowed house to be turned into home for her? (8,5)
14 This blooming neat view (2-3)
15 Total, as two wickets down? (3-3-3)
17 Jerk ran about investing money for capital (4,5)
19 Short slump, then it's right (5)
21 Quarter of red matter (8,5)
24 Innocence shown, as Scotsman's sent back English after check (7)
25 Side's written after a line (7)
26 Extraordinary place name in older novel, something magic about it? (10)
27 In such British weather, close of businesses immediately? (4)

DOWN

1 All at once during vacation slob switched between universities (5-5)
2 Items spotted including shoddy stuff, say (7)
4 Call for retirement, as rough sport introduced to basic weapon (5,4)
5 Tree, old plant, a third cut up (5)
6 Lady Macbeth's words, as the infernal dog's shown the door? (3,6,4)
7 A very unreliable chap put in two rounds to find green (7)
8 More should be done (4)
10 Here see dancing girls, before exposure to the limits? (6,7)
13 In principality, expression of dismay at overturned legislation (7,3)
16 Unwelcome house guest turning up, man wearing sheet (9)
18 Posh, donning suit in sale (7)
20 Mantra beginning to charm among element showing character in Europe (7)
22 Model putting one hand out (5)
23 Eat starters of green noodles and wasabi (4)

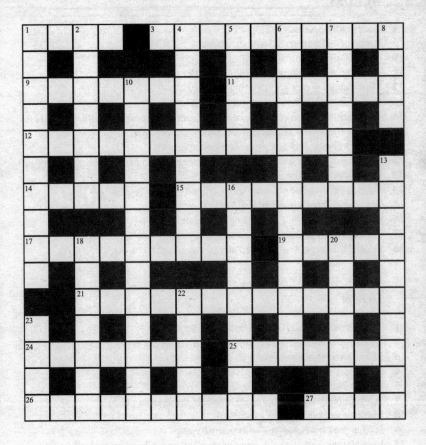

ACROSS

1 Course for horse races (8)
5 Result of rocket launch? (6)
10 Country singer, not very popular at first (5)
11 Bachelor maybe admitted going on Twitter (9)
12 Worry about secret agent getting in a stew (9)
13 Conservative leader with long memory (5)
14 A learner, for instance, being backward, needs support in school subject (7)
16 The heartless boss has sacked female computer expert (6)
18 Jalopies taking double bend at constant speed (6)
20 Mass taking place with archdeacon entering church (7)
22 Part of door in plane unhinged (5)
23 Studied PE — after training, took on head teacher's duties? (9)
25 We hear no beer's initially available at our local (9)
26 Don't censor anything about English comic (5)
27 Start again on problem, with extra energy (6)
28 Economist surprisingly named after a day of the week (8)

DOWN

1 Talk about problem with a therapist finally (8)
2 Hiding every now and then, man did fear snake (5)
3 Plant featured in Christmas gift guide? (4,2,9)
4 Ice cream, say, gobbled up by person on desert island? No way (7)
6 Officer likely to detain various cons etc (6,9)
7 I'm kept in by teacher, being thrashed for wrongdoing (4,5)
8 Itinerant worker about to join up (6)
9 Soldier perhaps belonging to extremist group? (6)
15 Republicans wanting soldiers to protect Reagan against racket? (9)
17 Announced yield given by my new investments (8)
19 Pathetic people shown how to make emergency call? (6)
20 Skipper's right to take Queen Elizabeth south of headland (7)
21 Key player, first to bat (6)
24 Large number engaged in class war, mostly (5)

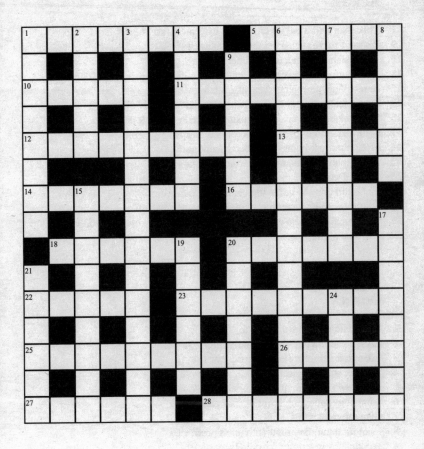

ACROSS

1 This chap will mess up father role extremely fast (4,3,7)
9 Refuse to give such a person bad character? (9)
10 Timepiece salesman left in diner (5)
11 It's a state old politician gets into (5)
12 Baseball player rejects dope after strong drinks (9)
13 Drunk leaves before time, crossing garden unevenly (4,4)
15 Steps taken when cricketer, losing wicket, gets duck (6)
17 Criminal with unlimited good or bad luck (6)
19 Setter thoroughly overwhelmed by ridicule? (8)
22 Tailor ignored note, making woman's coat (9)
23 Top dog's bite (5)
24 Eg Cavell dressed it, having bandages (5)
25 Spinning old lie about blokes being star-crossed (3-6)
26 One revealing cause of crash given fine (not heavy) by judge (6,8)

DOWN

1 Wait a moment as stud may do (4,4,6)
2 Bishop's following — over one million (7)
3 Changing sides for skin's getting raw (5)
4 Tougher soldiers given a lift on destroyer (8)
5 Like medal picked up for alcoholic drink (3-3)
6 Somebody following score in card game (6-3)
7 Give the right name … (7)
8 … of predator disturbed with one's prod? (8,6)
14 Woodchuck in corner, covered by earth (9)
16 Post-war new town's safe, sheltered area (8)
18 Affectionate term for female vet in US? Extremely respectful (3,4)
20 Intellectual made to support Labour leader (7)
21 Council's struggle in case of awful boozer (6)
23 Groom with love for jazz band (5)

ACROSS

1 She-goat that goes flying round the cathedral? (8)
5 From poles, with temperature dropping, one following series of peaks (6)
9 Gendarme allowed to arrest Frenchman for collaborating (9)
11 Short story being broadcast, a gripping one (5)
12 A small particle rotated, maintaining new state (7)
13 Emma's man speaking regularly (7)
14 Obsession with how Paris was before 1940? (13)
16 I warn athlete to detour around hard ground (5,4,4)
20 No traitor is a soft touch, needing a threesome to break (7)
21 Quantum number is too big to fix (7)
23 Picture that's splashed across glossy (5)
24 High priest speaking summons you to a table (9)
25 Receives a pair of waders, say, putting head inside (6)
26 Endlessly regret being captured by a Soviet type of brigade (8)

DOWN

1 Suited insect to cross river (6)
2 If this Athenian leaves an element, does any remain? (5)
3 Free from ordeal, taking every other comfort (7)
4 Part of Maastricht wrecked by parochial sect (6,7)
6 Colonist keen to speak in former British possession (7)
7 Game made in one diamond? (9)
8 Having an idea supporter on bike lacks class (8)
10 Cheat depressed by part of Oxford? It's hard to say (6-7)
14 Needlework moved into position outside (5,4)
15 Changing rooms at last at Times office (8)
17 Easy to see I have got over depression (7)
18 Mayhem commonly at a party — one's stoned (7)
19 Joined a team (6)
22 The middle of April, or earlier (5)

ACROSS

1 King going wild in Borneo (6)
5 Fence sheltering twin daughters having fun in pool? (8)
9 Exhaust in handy manner (8)
10 Roll over and discard small lump (6)
11 Mobile phone call about Monroe's last film (10)
13 What's to be done after this started? Seek an answer (4)
14 With more of a score, Pole becomes Pope (4)
15 Gendarme in riot not proceeding directly (10)
18 Throw in a religious medal (6,4)
20 Quote making sound sense (4)
21 State budget item taking thirty seconds (4)
23 Varying art form — source of easy money (5,5)
25 Punishable offence by leader of army in war zone (6)
26 Unfinished dessert otherwise identified as savoury dish (8)
28 Child's departure before reprehensible behaviour (6-2)
29 Bear close to river (6)

DOWN

2 Work of art like cobbler's last to be held in trust (3-6)
3 Bader's outfit is operational — no one draws? (7)
4 Non-existent flower seen endlessly (3)
5 Cartography lacking in part or parts of kingdom (5)
6 Put on hat to introduce main event at fête, perhaps (6,5)
7 Seafood criminal has left for start of meal (7)
8 Brad's collars (5)
12 Female governor's pot plant (6,5)
16 Suitable accommodation found in small ads? (3)
17 Pedant at first is tickled pink, interrupting slangy cop? (3-6)
19 Bury short article that's lacking compassion (7)
20 Ballet company, extremely excited, was unable to proceed on stage (7)
22 One's legless, and also holding sister up (5)
24 What's what for Burns, hoarding millions in capital? (5)
27 Trees said to provide exercise (3)

ACROSS

1 Capital head of industry invested in furniture (5)
4 Damage source of provisions, coming to old lady's feast (9)
9 Fail to heed wake-up call — past PM's making comeback! (9)
10 Man disturbed by girl's mode of expression (5)
11 Proper appeal for help by politicians making book (4,2,7)
14 Average bloke swallowing hallucinatory drug (4)
15 Extremely minor graduate reinvented as specialist in theatre (10)
18 Date of military action (10)
19 Unruffled state identified by millions (4)
21 Book of articles on vessel trapped in rock (5,3,5)
24 Bird hiding among summer leaves (5)
25 Member of society's real capital gain finally secured (9)
27 On which angels and devils may appear and Lady Godiva did? (9)
28 Introduce chips but no fish (5)

DOWN

1 Sportsperson penalised for a refusal to exhibit clothing (10)
2 Disapproving expression once regularly encountered in offices (3)
3 Help to make a bag-like structure, say? (6)
4 Line in great musician's mass producing state of confusion (9)
5 Copy army expert (5)
6 I worried about stupid person, one making us start (8)
7 Abigail, for one, diverts a man when working (11)
8 Not everyone's problem, by the sound of it (4)
12 His act is killing, prompting mirth in southern monarch! (11)
13 Dog is aware miner collapsed (10)
16 Moderate Russian fellows silence revolution in Kiev (9)
17 Distress a good farm bailiff up north (8)
20 Series of lectures on this is aimed in the right direction (6)
22 A large burden fails to finish a Scottish town (5)
23 Nursemaid a graduate hired to begin with (4)
26 Witty remark causing upset to piper's son (3)

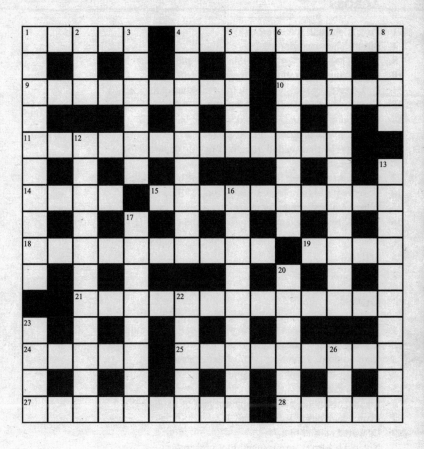

ACROSS

1 Principle single voice carries (5)
4 Bitter? Then consider salt (8)
8 Timely rule gone awry? I couldn't agree more! (5,7,2)
10 Bird taking lolly, tail first, to break perch (9)
11 Port seen from sea — it's only from the starboard side? (5)
12 Chaotic journey almost reaching capital (6)
14 Where one pays for the other doorbell to be fixed (8)
17 Denial, perhaps, among the people (8)
18 Train left behind second train, half having departed (6)
20 Hit a friend (5)
22 Communist I love, a revolutionary among holy people (9)
24 Observe pheasant, perhaps, being shot? (5,3,6)
25 Where nothing's right, typo said to be wrong (8)
26 Vertical line, for example, rotating around the side (1-4)

DOWN

1 Infernal machine run by German force in Europe (6,6)
2 Reliable note, for instance (5)
3 Herb used up, something with a joint one's eaten (9)
4 Heel — other end of foot cleaner? (6)
5 Link in story (8)
6 Finally, composer about to perform part of a sonata (5)
7 Plant which has to work in red (9)
9 Educated postie? (3,2,7)
13 Notable leader in government, fool in memoir (9)
15 Downhill slope, as God accepts shortcoming of colonial general (9)
16 Bound to limit exercise to roof (8)
19 River, over time, producing snapper (6)
21 Royal course taken by a Macbeth, say (5)
23 Rear not opening with old key (5)

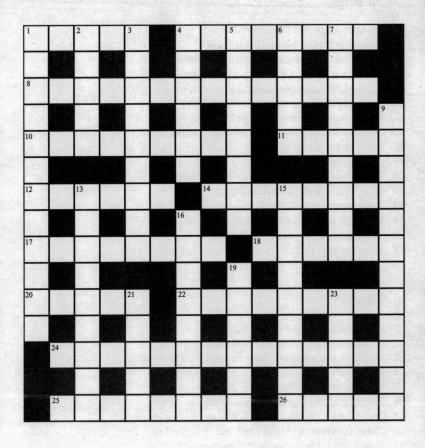

ACROSS

1 On lorry, chap loads fine food (9)
6 Subject to choose out of a thousand (5)
9 Stout cask trapped part of hand when withdrawn (7)
10 Freshwater creature with no power to come to land (7)
11 Sticker left by murder victim (5)
12 Complication from cold — doctor best for it (9)
14 Part of sea area breaks through (3)
15 Both Stalin and I condemned censor's verdict (5,6)
17 Perfume for the flush? (6,5)
19 Way to lose a stick (3)
20 Endlessly grave woodcutter, a resident of St Petersburg (3,6)
22 Like film, a stock production (5)
24 Rejected green jam? It's wizard (7)
26 Oven has brown hinged flap (7)
27 Composer puts brief pause before end of symphony (5)
28 In emergency, replace forty-odd booted out of university (2,4,3)

DOWN

1 Bone discovered in Roman villa (5)
2 Chest flat finally, in no way feminine (7)
3 Maintain around noon church is over? Disagree! (9)
4 Rude order to stand clear is unusual (3-2-3-3)
5 Little creature last to see paper (3)
6 Sort of card sharp pockets nothing (5)
7 In setting for orchestra, a fault turning over for player (7)
8 Politician speaking in the chair, full of himself (9)
13 Newly-treated boil completely removed (11)
14 Broken elbow that gets one off the rails perhaps (4,5)
16 Attractive 19 *ac* publication during Roses clash (3,6)
18 One million taken by gnome — that's wrong (7)
19 Censure work on raincoat? (7)
21 Board game occupied some sort of aunt (5)
23 Nurse's job not needing all that energy (5)
25 Sort of glove, a sort that has no name (3)

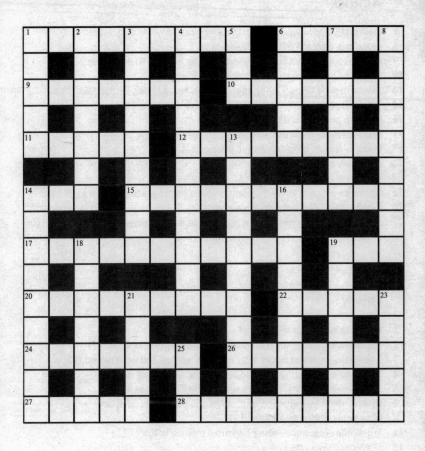

ACROSS

1 Relatively minor attack is repulsed by warship — victory at last! (10)
6 Guzzler's emptied wine bottle (4)
9 Giving report about company in recession moving to new premises (10)
10 Quite insignificant aspect of conflict in Yemen (4)
12 Minor trouble stirred up by Man U spectator: I'll join in (5,2,1,6)
14 I tried desperately to be more organised (6)
15 Chinese person's endless courage (8)
17 Have no time, unfortunately (8)
19 Food in part of hospital always rejected (6)
22 Play with best mate? (2,5,7)
24 Pal, shy when drunk? (4)
25 Sheltered by clergyman, little girl's given single portion of pasta (10)
26 Gossip about north American native (4)
27 Youngster, when claiming unemployment benefit, gets very little money (10)

DOWN

1 Father shows anger with son (4)
2 Between beginning and end of blizzard, transport's delayed (7)
3 In trouble, criminal leader gets arrested, judged and imprisoned (12)
4 Understand belonging to trade union's the very thing (6)
5 Takes flight, say, after turning up in part of airport (4,4)
7 Protest about introduction of revolutionary form of transport (7)
8 New pet is only a small dog (3,7)
11 We would ring, announcing beautiful women below? (7,5)
13 Way loyal associate keeps fighting to end of conflict? (10)
16 One initiating romance with girl at end of old-fashioned dance (8)
18 Ruddy criminal keeping lips sealed (7)
20 He wrote a new Morse novel (7)
21 Eel-like fish seen from side of boat (6)
23 007 character is seen at opening of this film (4)

absd

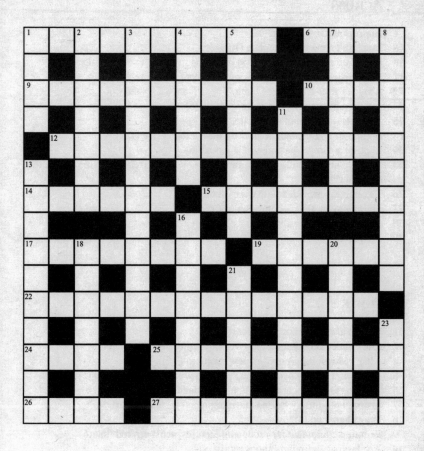

ACROSS

1 Appropriate indentation (4)
3 Displayed food put on a plate (10)
10 Rough up chap with a name (9)
11 Leave in a convenient place a hooded coat (5)
12 Anxious after Ann ripped cloth (7)
13 America invested in school and station (6)
15 Animals — deviants — deviated (9,6)
18 Composer and metaphysical poet, husband of Anne H? (7,8)
21 Idiot seen across one lake in the gloom (6)
23 A magician travelling west, I must go to Northern Ireland, taking couple to hospital (7)
26 Tutor Teddy provided with essay finally (5)
27 President's mother, a controller of Colorado (6,3)
28 Fruit began rolling around in wagon (10)
29 Letters man read out (4)

DOWN

1 Citizen accepting honour, in case (10)
2 Priest accepted criterion (5)
4 Alter fashion, incorporating new standard (3,6)
5 Member of family using bishop perhaps wins knight for pawn (5)
6 Showing no emotion, four left, leaving deadlock (7)
7 Instrument initially having alarming repercussions on girl (9)
8 Drag charge up (4)
9 Bringing equipment for producing pictures, artist arrived first (6)
14 Aimless, so I wander a shocking line (10)
16 Complaining wife supported by ruler (9)
17 Criminal bore hung — I will be next (9)
19 Bird may settle in any loch (7)
20 Hardy companion's bloomer (6)
22 You may be full of energy and mirth (2-3)
24 One preceding Juliet in the country (5)
25 Trade in wood (4)

ACROSS

1   Flight path … (9)
9   … making final approach? (7)
10 American uncle and a youngster knocked back liqueur (7)
11 Nothing done wrong in old theatre (5)
12 Kitchen utensil — a chopper (3-6)
13 They cover something new in ace pilot's qualification (7)
15 City where I'll take part in revolution (5)
17 Harassed communist removed evidence of membership (5)
18 Council's sincerity only on the outside? Show agreement (5)
19 Listened to quiet man on board (5)
20 Man with Arab connection, perhaps? (7)
23 Hide significant details of case, but getting sorted out (9)
25 Distance restricting northern children's author (5)
27 Mean to declare before a long time (7)
28 Funny comedian lacking energy for travelling (7)
29 Flight to be taken at a standstill? (9)

DOWN

1   Says team never has a coherent plan (6)
2   Old fellow supporting member in complete disaster (10)
3   Way to circumvent hindrance in risky venture (8)
4   Separate technique dad's introduced … (5)
5   … stay to demonstrate it (9)
6   Isolate distress signal (6)
7   Refer to crummy dive (4)
8   In the past, maybe Kelly has accepted one's suffering (8)
14 Note on monotonous song about LA? That's cool! (10)
16 Succeed in delivering new issue? (9)
17 Soon to appear suitably elegant (8)
18 Market to be entered by former tennis star, one that's washed up? (8)
21 Woman gathering information for items to be discussed (6)
22 One burning out on a high? (6)
24 Composer finally lost part of his income (5)
26 When first of colleagues retires, rise in branch (4)

41

ACROSS

1 Very loud ringing in E sharp (10)

6 Nod and release voucher (4)

10 Pride in the past, encapsulated by short quote (7)

11 Transfer is boost for players (7)

12 Enter clubs in high spirits clutching French wine goblet (6,3)

13 Rum punch, conclusively fine end to party! (5)

14 Informal sort of relations today between old and young, initially (5)

15 Attack hollow feature projecting reactionary books (5,4)

17 Have to go back to one's ladies, perhaps speaking with nobleman (4,5)

20 Somewhere for those with bills to settle? (5)

21 Ultimately loath to yank you from bunk (5)

23 Dressed down, saving large bonnet for the first time in one's life (9)

25 Author's hurried notes kept separate by FA (7)

26 Ulster's second row opening holdall, slowly revealing shiny new top? (7)

27 Fly from the Ark, for one mile (4)

28 One's carried up bouquet displaying different colours (10)

DOWN

1 Forthright in argument, but not instrumental (5)

2 Entitled to have these disappointments (but not statutory) (3-6)

3 Old air base has lawn, poor in parts, like muck? (8,6)

4 Crown, supporting judge, gets force to reduce charges? (4-3)

5 Turn to get drinks, taking pint up in the event (4-3)

7 He escapes whipping with old rope (5)

8 Creep one of a pair booted on stage? (9)

9 Gets out welcome wine and beers in National Park (9,5)

14 Measure: one that would end life on Mars some say (9)

16 Coin in eg loose change (9)

18 Sort of bomb with uranium going up in clouds? (7)

19 Land in debt after raising something for one's retirement (4,3)

22 Ball going under bottom of park boundary fencing (5)

24 What computing enthusiasts do for one, say (5)

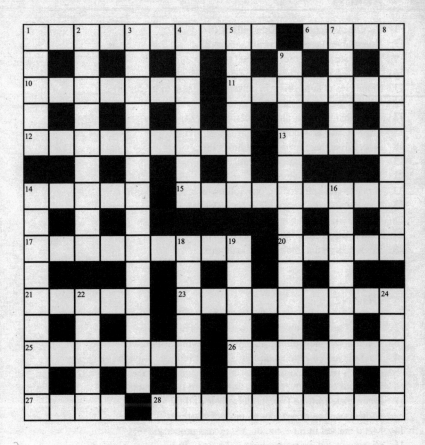

ACROSS

1 Return in support of sudden attack (6)
5 Beer pub brought back is for author (8)
9 Improvised reason for mistrial? (4-6)
10 A medic has turned in final piece of work (4)
11 Supporter of something in newspaper he tore to pieces (8)
12 Covering up corporal punishment (6)
13 Amphibian, in confusion, crossing river (4)
15 Most delicious wine in trial (8)
18 A bit of baggage from legal actions (8)
19 Rabbit caught by bowler, perhaps (4)
21 Some tack — it's cheesy (6)
23 A poet's work, including one volume that's repellent (8)
25 Panorama that's very wide at the sides (4)
26 Notes alarming changes to one area (10)
27 Man travels round British Isles (8)
28 Region as turned over to local ruler (6)

DOWN

2 Piece of boxing ring (5)
3 Fighter, very new plane, finally included in Air Force unit (9)
4 Having worked hard as diplomat, finally reduced friction (6)
5 Doctor's work providing meaningful options, in other words (6,9)
6 Religious type converted this unfortunate sailor first (8)
7 Incomplete fortune I had collected? It's all there (5)
8 Unit's invading one Asian country or another (9)
14 Metal is used in rake, to adopt standard procedure (9)
16 Bizarre instances happening all the time (9)
17 Deeply understood fellow Democrat embracing party (8)
20 Negligent, so fail again in one's aim? (6)
22 Broadcaster swore atrociously — what could be worse? (5)
24 Announcement when showing artwork in Eastern state (5)

ACROSS

1 Set boundaries for country, but ignore the north (6)
4 Heralds beginning to proclaim new decrees (8)
10 What baby needs — a little song? (7)
11 Bite with anger, being cross (7)
12 I succeeded ahead of trouble-maker (4)
13 Novel solution to piano-player's problem? (4-6)
15 Wife warning about danger of being hit in home in rural area (3,6)
16 Stick made of woody stuff and iron primarily (5)
18 One fish and second fish (5)
19 It could be cricket mates after play having a drink (4,5)
21 Plant needing help in mud, I suspect (10)
23 Screen in room lifted back (4)
26 Give a rough idea of forbidden policy (7)
27 One sticking salmon in middle of freezer for surgeon to eat (7)
28 Like a perpetual drunk catching cold from 18, say? (8)
29 Object when someone forgets party and fuss around front of house (6)

DOWN

1 Guided to the top to overlook huge island (5)
2 Cry of surprise about a river vessel crossing ocean (9)
3 Gospel not the first book in Bible (4)
5 Being most imprudent, the woman's taken in by scoundrel (7)
6 Dull firm needing to smile more? (10)
7 Putting energy into work in garden, end in pain having to stoop (5)
8 Flavour that's minute in repast badly prepared (9)
9 Tom wants Eastern goddess (6)
14 Non-Christian believer could be holiest type almost (10)
15 What happens when band becomes bad and tries to impress (4-5)
17 Vigorous old female laid into deviant (3-6)
19 Singers vocalised notes (7)
20 Stars gathered together in Italian city (6)
22 Game in which drunk loses head (5)
24 Time for Jo's family to appear (5)
25 Nothing is picked up — nothing that's on the floor (4)

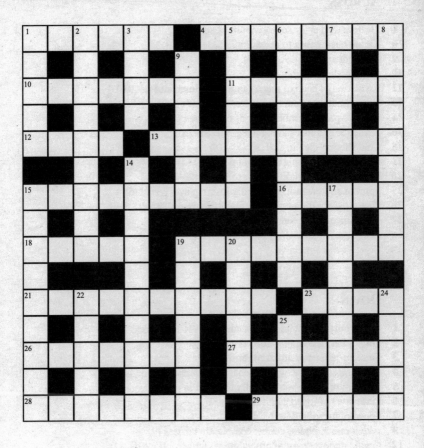

ACROSS

1 I follow wild crocuses after start of spring (9)
6 Knock back wines to get wobbly (5)
9 Frequent answer in search (5)
10 Art's model, possibly (3,6)
11 Escalation of a small flap to an international storm? (9,6)
13 Special hotelier with the Queen's drink (8)
14 Frantic spasm after brief cry of frustration (6)
16 Audience member having a jug after six (6)
18 Cold shower startling all of NSW (8)
21 Regardless of having no social position (15)
23 Reckless troublemaker, game to impress? (9)
25 Sportsman's captain, repeatedly losing player's lead (5)
26 Play on visit around middle of August (5)
27 Stoicism, a creed nun revived (9)

DOWN

1 To the north, British India's leader owns local address (5)
2 Forged bar: it contains iron (11)
3 Some in Jobcentre attacked request (7)
4 Glaswegian, maybe without charge and unpunished (4-4)
5 Problem in flash photo initially exposed in colour again (3-3)
6 Pixie lovers flipped a bit (7)
7 Speed reduced in desert ... (3)
8 ... *that* one in photo, almost completely lawless (9)
12 Legal handover's usual procedure no longer followed? (11)
13 Drawn into dumps for retirement years? (9)
15 After training, a student understood (8)
17 I've refined taste before engaging self-righteous copper (7)
19 Meanders over evacuated town near Eton (7)
20 Dodge unknown end of ride after yell from roller coaster? (6)
22 More than half of superb Cheddar, say (5)
24 22 seen regularly in spring (3)

ACROSS

1 Gold fixed in trees that needed flushing out (6,7)
9 Worn out in endless attempts to save time (5)
10 Confidence in what may follow life (9)
11 No more discussion when it's time to close the book (3,2,5)
12 Rule about start of lunch that may consist of many courses (4)
14 Be behind counter in bank, in great style (7)
16 Through Scottish island soldier is about to charge (7)
17 Secure attention, closing British licensed premises (4,3)
19 Man investigating responses to a meringue (7)
20 Cut round one circle and another (4)
21 Defendant's taken in to mass, as usual (10)
24 To be a model, I pose — time to change (9)
25 Confused? Worse things can happen here (2,3)
26 Unapproachable sort of freak gadget (6,7)

DOWN

1 Direct product of Welsh factories (2,3,4,5)
2 Association Football ultimately accepted by good Scots (5)
3 One in a suit seen in finest social venue (3,2,5)
4 Nervous about skin growth that's dark (7)
5 Old empire, so small, insubstantial to overturn (7)
6 One gets up early for a bit of fun (4)
7 So detained an ocean-going fighter briefly in place with no coast (3,6)
8 Book course after end of year, with some earlier months abroad (7,3,4)
13 Easy money from one stock option exercise? (5,5)
15 Roughly ignore old waterman (9)
18 Confirmation of purchase of extremely rare chair, say (7)
19 Composer making arrangement for couple added note in (7)
22 No tenderness at first in Mr Scrooge (5)
23 Sheep having nothing to eat wander off (4)

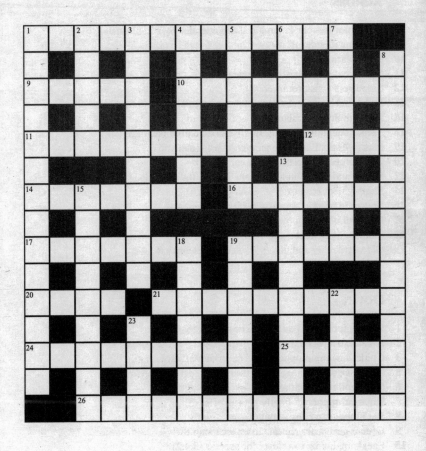

ACROSS

1 Minimum number of female sheep attended by vet, ultimately (6)
4 Hidden cur bodes ill (8)
10 Gypsy fare? (9)
11 Somewhat genre-busting puzzle (5)
12 Simpleton's stick returned (3)
13 Drama film, or Gertrude Atherton's original novel (5,6)
14 Rumour about harbour (6)
16 Favour daughter entering English and another language (7)
19 Favour lifted York-born painter, briefly involved (7)
20 One's regular date, not easily excited (6)
22 Helpless victim of con trick swallowing Italian dodge (7,4)
25 Employ trick to get rid of leader (3)
26 Ill, losing head in depression (5)
27 Car pool is turning out to be a high point (9)
28 Sloth, say, attendee suffered (8)
29 Old Greek coin and note pocketed by celebrity (6)

DOWN

1 Shrine, substantial one ahead of scholar (6)
2 American cowboys, those in dispute (9)
3 Guide showing prophet round heart of marketplace (5)
5 US dance director following tradition in part of Mayfair (8,6)
6 Shell trolley on hilltop (9)
7 Fanatical supporter finally gets an offer (5)
8 Rat in waste, rolling about (8)
9 Officer gets near criminal after escape (6,8)
15 Speak up, but be too clever for success (3,4,2)
17 Fish reportedly studied on Hebridean island by European leader of team (3,6)
18 Jam in pupil's first book (8)
21 Tricky question: given time to relax, start to reply (6)
23 Set up short key ceasefire (5)
24 Ram a truck's rear wheels and this could be broken (5)

ACROSS

1 City mostly welcoming to English — until now! (10)
6 On which a boxer may be chief performer (4)
10 Spat excessively on radio receiver to begin with (3-2)
11 Old boy in Paris who sees about funeral rites (9)
12 Lookalike with money set out in this sort of jacket (6-8)
14 This writer's associated with a rebel school (7)
15 Person demonstrating energy in springtime run (7)
17 Tree planted by American conductor (7)
19 Get in touch with permit to make lock (7)
20 This posy's on the ground — it requires chlorophyll (14)
23 Created opening around front of reef (coral) (9)
24 Go mad, struggling in teaching (5)
25 Time to return, disturbed by queen's mews (4)
26 Mint coin — sovereign, possibly (10)

DOWN

1 Publican's spirit that's no good (4)
2 Philosophy getting Lear into a mess (9)
3 He may fix problem with horn, securing hard cash first (14)
4 Like ground meal, we're told? Fancy! (7)
5 Where one may spout rubbish about son's spirit (7)
7 One of two writers turning material over (5)
8 Facts about monarch receiving team? They're what's wanted (10)
9 Flying officer 'S'? He's superior in rank (8,6)
13 Feeble chap put up by doctor breaking foot (5-5)
16 Stop one at a time, heading off with hesitation (9)
18 Female European at centre of dancing (7)
19 Viscous substance upset on youngster's dress fabric (7)
21 Instruct bachelor to get out of bed (5)
22 Bouncer is ruddy short (4)

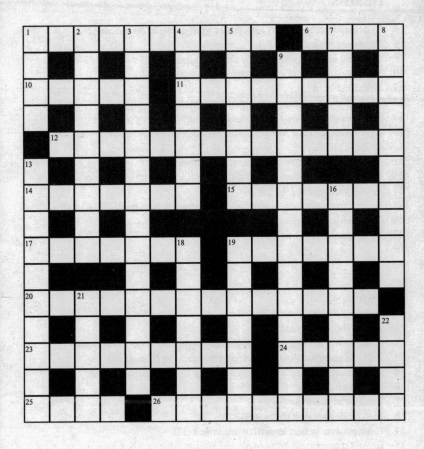

ACROSS

1 Courtesy in competition with leader giving way to companion (8)
5 Governor settled strike (6)
9 Troubled and overwhelmed by utter annulment (8)
10 Facility in middle of district creating problem (6)
12 Wobbling hard (5)
13 Washed less than enthusiastically initially in youth (9)
14 Schemes in a bad way to restrict current smooth progress (5,7)
18 Reveals money, last bit in wallet, carried in hands initially for short distance (5-7)
21 Carelessly wound, thin yarn unravelled finally? (9)
23 Hit opening with British cast (5)
24 Soldiers understanding test (6)
25 Degree to which there's attachment of silly labels in sport (8)
26 Open with apprehension of resistance, annoyed (6)
27 Most appropriately free at end of life span (8)

DOWN

1 Secret about past time (6)
2 Behaviour that's stupid and unfriendly stopped by one in party (6)
3 Bulbous plant's soft area, overturned, receiving damage (9)
4 Defiant one in court with angry speech following memory mostly (12)
6 Exist with purpose? Correct (5)
7 Prop water bottle up (8)
8 Map grid, a revised pattern (8)
11 Confirm aunt is best at getting organised (12)
15 Cross set up outside front of shrine after suggestion? Not hard (9)
16 Son greeting daughter before personal confrontation (8)
17 Muddle is admitted by blushing staff, upset (8)
19 Principle I displayed in support of mother country (6)
20 Case nearly over apart from marginal features put aside (6)
22 Treatment from university authority (5)

ACROSS

1   Scale of disaster getting more costly over time (7)
5   Expert has photo after photo cropped (7)
9   Row with a German agitated financial official (4,7)
10 Part of face, like cheek (3)
11 Pole may have this large bottle (6)
12 Perfect female, impossible to control? (8)
14 Books etc in university town are important (7,6)
17 Union, initially, started by nonconformist of old school (5,8)
21 Soldier perhaps, one lad guarding daughter for personal protection (8)
23 Measure of power within a circle backed in capital (6)
25 Cut ends off with single blow (3)
26 For example, army uniform found in this accommodation (7,4)
27 Not a subject that's rewarding for a writer (7)
28 Some fraud I torpedo? (7)

DOWN

1   Turn off fan initially on (6)
2   Part of Roman army almost catching a mythical creature (7)
3   Party more reformed? Not for long (9)
4   Sovereign together with African money (4)
5   Points out Oxford Street illuminations (10)
6   Bowled unfairly right into middle of the wicket (5)
7   Disturbed the soil that's most sacred (7)
8   Records shot resulting in a hanging (8)
13 Dry soldier, oddly, as drunk's frequent companion (10)
15 A role he and I had in divisive policy (9)
16 One who inspires the rest (8)
18 After gate change, direction for flight (7)
19 Distribute information in part of plant (7)
20 Fellow-player that contributes to a result (6)
22 Remove water from vessel containing small plant (5)
24 Location of listed building one's entering every year (4)

ACROSS

1 Confirmed Roman couple have caught cold in kidneys etc (8)
5 Lead around garden English girl (6)
8 Crowd in novel raises attendant up (3,7)
9 Extremely slick, bidding team to change direction suddenly (4)
10 A king in Ireland's wish, strangely, to be part of Scotland (5,3,6)
11 Uneven square isn't army land (7)
13 Wide boy's a gossip! (7)
15 Dirt acquired on school dunce (7)
18 Had no managerial duties when pursuing true power and a voice (7)
21 Badly crippled, but one is serving the community (6-8)
22 Police statement informing of damage (4)
23 Finish rest and run after day becomes warmer (10)
24 Initially, sixth former after college for boys and girls (6)
25 Recalling modest accommodation, not forthcoming about too much (8)

DOWN

1 Authorities could make topless bar close (7)
2 US city rep's top duo breaking into Flower of Scotland (4,5)
3 Is a pot-boiler still produced by this romantic novelist? (7)
4 Pigmy, not native to the west, hiding opposite (7)
5 Food and drink upset over one breaking into cab meter (9)
6 After a fashion show's start, phone in centre keeps ringing (2,5)
7 I never did take away millions in live shows! (5,2)
12 Creature in white coat and bow tie nearly caught throw (6,3)
14 Amusing article out of place — ever an obsession (9)
16 Roughly fixed pin to accompanying message (7)
17 Able to get about a shilling for decorations (7)
18 Champion wrestling, having boxed before (7)
19 Danger increasing tenfold, finally turned to stone (7)
20 Arranged men at great expense: a failing (7)

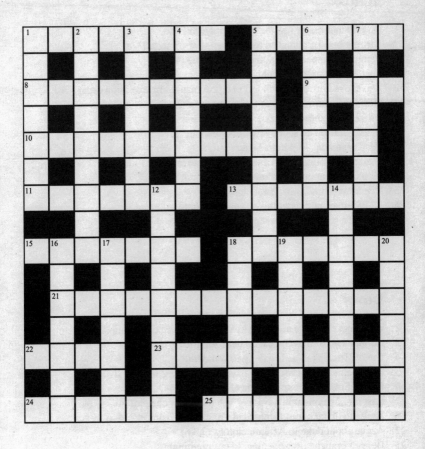

51

ACROSS

1 Pass up mountain, say, the wrong way (8)
9 Turning briefly, managed to reverse — who's to tell? (8)
10 Being small, meeting another small being (4)
11 Lost it (the war, presumably) ... (5,1,6)
13 ... as those born in Tripoli left one year, caught by exclusion order (6)
14 Ship's welcoming party to make you strip (3,5)
15 Good times ahead? A man's into past events (7)
16 Good, and sort of short, WW2 campaign (7)
20 Very beaten up — what a boxer (8)
22 Caretaker around front of tee getting hole in one (6)
23 Man City's set out to follow United without a plan (12)
25 Drink in the end is to irritate church (4)
26 Fit in nurses with opening of sanatorium (8)
27 Sugar's a remarkable remedy — back it (8)

DOWN

2 Unfairness of leave admitted by one with desire to turn up (8)
3 Copper's heart may appear so delicate (6-6)
4 Cut off from France, is having to wander (8)
5 One seems to see everything from hill covering wide area (4-3)
6 Front of tractor has spiked wheel for digger (6)
7 Last bit of payment in advance? What's left of cheque? (4)
8 Agree to differ about fish hauled up, subject to debate? (4,4)
12 Argue about duke in African clothes (3,3,6)
15 Begged branch, after opening, to cut premium (8)
17 Estate with monument announced for where Gordon fell (8)
18 Staff run round before finding stray (8)
19 Did stroke exercise and died, overcome (7)
21 Regular guys? (6)
24 Decline to drink (4)

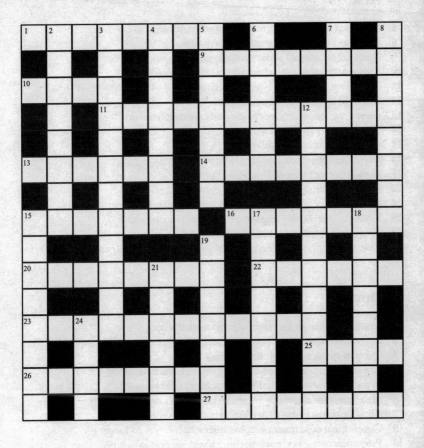

ACROSS

1 Guard taking action to provide protection for old-timer (9)
6 Shock as saint enters church property? (5)
9 One's contemptuous about ecology party, no good in revolution (7)
10 Single despicable character in film such as Hook? (7)
11 Tour in resort, taking eastern direction (5)
12 Grumble about a part song (9)
13 Feature of Indian cuisine fellow finds almost Greek (8)
14 United striker overturned ban (4)
17 Girl's not extremely sophisticated (4)
18 Driver perhaps drinks nothing — unlike me? (8)
21 Islander's cruel remark wounding Diana (9)
22 Fail resit? Here are the odds, to begin with (5)
24 David's boy, a born dancer with no end of aptitude (7)
25 Trying to stop family members taking part in card game (7)
26 Like a match, perhaps, likely to flare up? (5)
27 Colour of duck, say, on easternmost edges of Lake Michigan (4,5)

DOWN

1 German runner getting stitch again when climbing (5)
2 Daily newspaper over a pound? Thus price increases appear novel (3,3,4,5)
3 Rider in storm nears home shortly (8)
4 In a stage musical, criminally treat versatile performers (8)
5 In part of EU once elected representative's held sway (6)
6 Male reluctant ultimately to enter exam? One's only human (6)
7 Conscription possibly viewed as antisocial? Never (8,7)
8 Government department keeping queen in comfort no longer (9)
13 Priest officiating in church needing to get support in fast (9)
15 Fellow consumer turned up in party at pub with air conditioning (8)
16 Name of German boy band fronted by lady-killer (8)
19 See friend swallowing drug for depression (6)
20 Some engaged in 7 remain unsettled (6)
23 Cross borne by Antigone (5)

ACROSS

1 Answered note received by the extremely wealthy diplomat (10)
7 Plead with one wielding knife to spare son (4)
9 Set aside what I did after a let (8)
10 Goodbye? I'm back! (Stalks over the floor) (6)
11 Man of religion finally changes into cotton (6)
13 Some tobacco large guy chewed, very unattractive (4-4)
14 Shoot young birds — have a swallow (4,3,5)
17 Fight, and what ends it, in the old rhyme (4,4,4)
20 Songbird's short length in question (8)
21 Get on top of animal to ford river (6)
22 Gloss paint smeared over area (6)
23 Case, one vital bag held back (8)
25 As water bird, what dipper does round end of beach (4)
26 Go over to college in part of London (5,5)

DOWN

2 Will I deal with manager? I've ignored junior men (8)
3 Secure a match (3)
4 Bird very small in close-up? Yes and no (5)
5 Swimmer so able to touch bottom, as detailed (2-5)
6 Current issue thus off the press, though not picked up (3,6)
7 Like some Indians' sacred cow? (11)
8 Film actor hugs maiden in punt (6)
12 Movement in formation of study I put up in school (4,7)
15 Perhaps Richard III's intuition gets support (9)
16 Speech sounds the Spanish composer used under pressure (8)
18 Alight, I daren't move (7)
19 Cover provides warmth in silence (6)
21 The ball to get us out, say? (5)
24 It may cover the road and nearly the lake (3)

ACROSS

1 Imagine daughter touching cat's back (5,2)
5 Inch quietly away from dust cloud following quake (7)
9 Lover or partner to bolt food (3)
10 Folding leaf's mechanical partition (5,6)
11 A disadvantage going in with a cold-blooded killer (8)
12 US city organised workers' zone in centre (6)
15 Irishman seeing nothing odd in devotion (4)
16 Resentment about worry's sort of novel (10)
18 With time, delivers sound anti-inflationary measure (4-6)
19 With ink one's maybe filled in form (4)
22 Broadcaster that's first-rate and free (6)
23 Parent and kid about to pocket one grand (8)
25 Feeling less pressure, once Reg is here (6-5)
27 Some tea? Don't bother! (3)
28 Strike's backing so firm in Mexican province (7)
29 Bananas, more than anything, in a turnover stopping appetite! (7)

DOWN

1 Almost comic live action hero (3,4)
2 Maiden over of superior quality (5,6)
3 I stand on this bunk! (2,4)
4 Big shot with mansion and a chauffeur (4-6)
5 For audience, interpret a piece for organ (4)
6 One taking snaps enjoys the flowers (8)
7 Drawing conclusions from ultra superior argument (3)
8 Old men swimming with energy daily across channel (2,5)
13 Standard charge to pen French that's appropriate (11)
14 Artist buzzing round China cut short a great show (10)
17 Condition associated with elegance? Not quite (8)
18 Bats want to flourish, finally building stand (7)
20 Yank, heading off, gets striking win, by chance (4,3)
21 Humble and desperate measure again used in extremes (6)
24 Capable of working at till (2,2)
26 Press dismiss second book of mine, then reflect (3)

ACROSS

1 Into the part, Monroe finally signed name (10)
6 Run in the opposite direction, seeing philanderer (4)
10 Head off without a regular income, forever young (7)
11 Deceptive action, but backfiring before one working (7)
12 First from Mondrian, or a trend that's off-the-wall, might it be? (6,3)
13 Each jolly on last of booze (5)
14 Project outlining invasion's ending with a military leadership (5)
15 Athlete's back as sore as one from Bow, say (9)
17 Come down on meek type popping pill, the fool (9)
20 Idea producing point against our rivals? (5)
21 Lid changed on something preserved that tastes good! (5)
23 Pint is drunk, less (not litre) for insobriety (9)
25 PM's predecessor entertaining friend in yuppie, perhaps (7)
26 Young swimmer given a little stick (7)
27 Pull one across the pond (4)
28 Jokers may be so after award, given English wit (5,5)

DOWN

1 Lover's first between the sheets in field (5)
2 Twenty-five-pound envelope for returned subscription, grand for another title (9)
3 Life yet to come together, and dissolute, Turkish governor claimed (3,5,6)
4 Opera, overtures to *Lohengrin* and *Ernani* seen in proportion (2,5)
5 Electra's brother could be so terse (7)
7 Old fruit producer, sheepish? (5)
8 Want for nothing, not being in love (5-4)
9 Opening investigation has fix involving match that was painful! (8,6)
14 Sweet little setter? (5,4)
16 Fuel line under sink I lose in a tangle (6,3)
18 Time among group of women without husband — one's a virgin (7)
19 A hot temperature with hot pot set up, which is flammable (7)
22 Wally has a busier schedule, they say (5)
24 View causing argument (5)

ACROSS

1 Meet cyclists at first at side of road (8)
5 Believe this is a decent exam grade (6)
9 One putting the frighteners on soldier out of condition (9)
11 US city reveals plan to back fast road (5)
12 Original setting for Mozart opera, lacking loud tune? The reverse (7)
13 Locks lunatic inside? That's not natural (3-4)
14 Half hope, after entering employment, to get a pension (8,5)
16 Constrained by tight budget, old architect's forced to resign (2,1,10)
20 Spanish hotel staff about to meet one coming by plane? (7)
21 What you see on roads, eg signs for *Car Park* and *Stop* (7)
23 Claude's endlessly drunk as a lord? (5)
24 Figure in the Tory reshuffle (6,3)
25 Old shepherd taking step towards peak (6)
26 Memory's a big worry at first for physicist (8)

DOWN

1 Whip used by largely merciless member of medieval sect (6)
2 Rules in court, most ignored quite regularly (5)
3 Raised a flag after capturing rebel leaders in African country (7)
4 Danger — Britain under attack! Keep stiff upper lip (4,3,4,2)
6 The first to retire to the country don't speak the language (7)
7 Theatre producer not quite ready to wear women's clothing (9)
8 One attempting to embrace me, last to wait in line (8)
10 Protest about Tommy's initial allowance after battle (13)
14 Supporters suppressing bad language, mostly, in sporting events (4,5)
15 Stupid dope involved in military takeover gets imprisoned (6,2)
17 Spanish fellow so glad I had picked up cases (7)
18 One English workers' group's supporting police force (7)
19 Group of pupils stumped right at start of test? That's not unknown (6)
22 American/British affair (5)

ACROSS

1 Briefly communicate with a national leader like LBJ (5)
4 Inflated device planted by a 16, with nothing lost (9)
9 Marsupials welcoming pit's abundance of space (9)
10 It beats the name of a prison in Midlothian! (5)
11 Woman who's become murder victim? (6)
12 Abandon offspring at end of pier, say (8)
14 Society member not even sad about unfinished material … (9)
16 … thus digests book about Zeno of Citium, perhaps (5)
17 Browser heading for electric light (5)
19 Current side meets another, securing runs (9)
21 Yield, accepting wine with directions in case (8)
22 Paternal grandmother injected with last of hospital's blood fluid (6)
25 Criminal activity vicar ignored at first (5)
26 Bizarre origins an Italian girl revealed (9)
27 Pearly king's merchandise finally presented as offer (4,5)
28 Senior member longing to attend social gathering (5)

DOWN

1 Revolutionary way to display shock when late? (4,2,4,5)
2 Cattle-rearer in South Africa has ox running wild (5)
3 Greenness of first-class surgeon in Northumberland (7)
4 Drink queen possibly had on river (4)
5 Defeat argument over Bartok's last magnum opus (10)
6 Bill loathes Aeneas's faithful friend (7)
7 Teaches one lacking model to play in different key (9)
8 Abundant supply reduced — with what? (3-3-4-5)
13 Foolish ladies lived out East in disorderly state (3-7)
15 Doing as one's ordered, coming to this conclusion (9)
18 Thaw in relations revealed by woman swigging wine (7)
20 Permitted to set up crossing, he built the Menai bridge (7)
23 Skinned like mole without having ears (5)
24 A freshwater fish used in making soups? (4)

ACROSS

1 I'm surprised lettuce is getting fungal disease (7)
5 A saint, out and about like his adversary (7)
9 Food given endless praise — put in very small cooker, needing little time (3-2-4)
10 Frighten someone with weapon who's no good (5)
11 Bombast from grand fellow going around with one clique getting drunk (13)
13 At least three women, it seems, getting illnesses (8)
15 Wine demonstrating excellence? Look for one! (6)
17 Some science work given marks, we hear (6)
19 Craftsman has hesitation — one not getting on with the job? (8)
22 Often Derek is so kind (6-7)
25 Aquino elected — some woman! (5)
26 Chemical attractor that could give one more hope with women ultimately? (9)
27 Understanding of English shown with this writer's gripping passage? (7)
28 Writer's fate, being hauled back with yarn not right (7)

DOWN

1 Run? Maiden over lacks that (4)
2 White powder — shout when it spreads around the 'ouse? (7)
3 Robbed and tied up, with burglar finally escaping (5)
4 Remarkable fellows taking out gangster — a few drops of blood here? (8)
5 Attacks succeeded — messages sent up to convey that (4,2)
6 Scripture undermines culture that's degenerate and aggressive (9)
7 Token number, the smallest amount, completely inadequate (7)
8 Guess there may be a sort of therapy in magic (10)
12 Bring in one of an earlier generation, not half bringing weight (10)
14 Reduction in one type of sleep in satisfactory surroundings (9)
16 Bond may be in love — can't get excited (8)
18 A number drink audibly and become edgy (5,2)
20 Survive the sound of mocking scepticism (4,3)
21 Irritable fellow who may want a good deal (6)
23 Possibly a monster fish (5)
24 Tax? There's high spirits, seeing it abolished (4)

ACROSS

1 Part-time medic (4)
3 Place to sit and have food after operating system (6,4)
9 Greek character embracing a lively dance (7)
11 Erect university, to acclaim (7)
12 Down-to-earth, like poet's cats (9)
13 Publish volume about part of early education (5)
14 Composer mainly helping decision-making process (12)
18 The law broken on open land in Australia, say (12)
21 Scientific device one sitting idly mentioned (5)
22 Right to enter guilty plea, perhaps (9)
24 Had shot in the air and caused some damage (7)
25 Rodents make mess originally in cereal (7)
26 Paper money that's needed for survival (5,5)
27 Postpone visit (4)

DOWN

1 Is first across border where some aircraft come down (8)
2 Bad male band, really bad (8)
4 Sacrificial offering replaced in part of OT account (5)
5 Old garment being worn by King and Queen of hearts, say (9)
6 A couple of typos in work, professor? Easily corrected with this (4,9)
7 Bring out drug in conformance with law (6)
8 Score with little time left before close of play (6)
10 Nobody else can write this, truly (13)
15 Sign addition to law imprisoning a robber (3-6)
16 Having corrected tailspin, one climbs (8)
17 Court is uncertain about monarch (8)
19 Tranquil head of clan in Highland dress (6)
20 Taking part in mass, is in saint's birthplace (6)
23 Charming woman, 15's assistant (5)

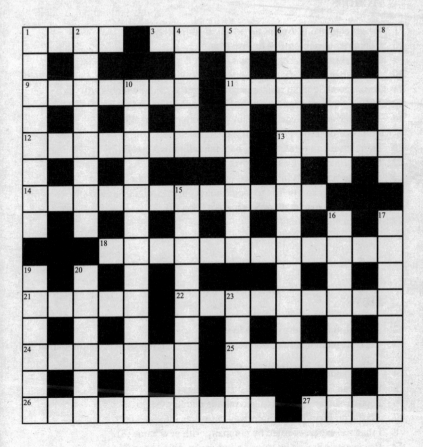

ACROSS

1 Writer supporting American president ultimately (6)
5 Container used by sailor for fish (8)
9 Salesgirl in Loire area is useless (8)
10 Game abandoned after a daughter's back injury (6)
11 Announced Scottish runner is not among the medal winners? (6)
12 Little sign of movement in group after leader's ousted (8)
14 They may supply a drug to man with tooth problem (12)
17 Influence of traffic cops? (7,5)
20 Step thus taken by clergyman backing religious festival (8)
22 I could be choked by swirling cigarette smoke (6)
23 One planting seeds interrupted by onset of heavy rain (6)
25 Middle East experts first to look into reconstruction of Basra? (8)
26 Piece in newspaper about Steptoe And Son (8)
27 Poor friend gets shot (6)

DOWN

2 Animal, full of energy, broke loose (6)
3 Conduct ineffective election campaign, say, in temporary accommodation? (5,6)
4 Try to land (9)
5 European journalist in smart surroundings (7)
6 Popular singer opposed to leaving the country (5)
7 Traffic problem just at motorway entrances (3)
8 Financial expert enlisted by company with new name (8)
13 Being extremely eager to go on holiday, packing case (11)
15 Dodgy dealer one means to pay punctually (4,5)
16 British consumer saving hard for time off work (8)
18 Food and wine in short supply in distant lands (3,4)
19 Badger runs to bottom of steep ground (6)
21 French author never appearing in translation (5)
24 Pay cut? He must be joking (3)

ACROSS

1 Church group's Oedipus complex (4,3)
5 Turner surpasses Brown (7)
9 One's expelled from school, then given a placement and passed over (9)
10 Company having bad time in recession (5)
11 Swimmer in school with American astronomer (5)
12 Gardener worried about old instrument (4,5)
14 Concur that post going astray is unsatisfactory (3,2,2,7)
17 Unfinished business also includes disgusting musical work (8,6)
21 Wise man — one from northern Europe — developed a rash (9)
23 Clergyman ultimately wanting page three, for example (5)
24 Cricket side prepared for attack (5)
25 Goofy one's left bone dry (9)
26 Where children may play with spades and where men may work with picks (7)
27 One can't resist cricketer, needing new opener (7)

DOWN

1 Capital engineer turning up in middle of road (6)
2 Retrospective, to some extent, for a mature artist of the floating world (7)
3 Row with outsiders in race being held in low esteem (9)
4 Playwright dropping pence says truckers may use them (11)
5 Not real fish (3)
6 King Edward, say, dismissing a primate (5)
7 Half of them being made redundant — anything considered (7)
8 Article supporting New English writer that caused sorrow to be forgotten (8)
13 Sergeant may revert to former state (4,7)
15 River trip must include old family member (3,6)
16 One not coming out promises to pay for plant (8)
18 For a Swedish soprano, nothing's like this nightingale's debut (7)
19 Work out what heir apparent should do (7)
20 Sheltered spot occupied by small tanker (6)
22 What about ram getting agitated? (3,2)
25 Save clumsy boat that's overturned (3)

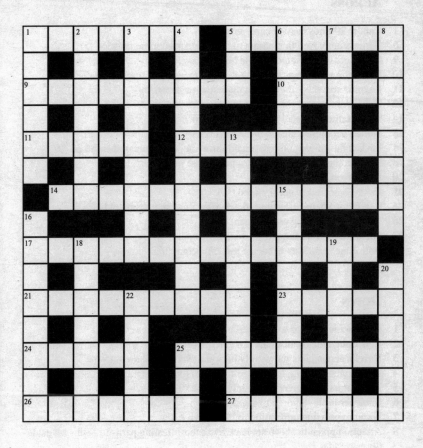

ACROSS

1   Candle 20 finds easy to carry around (9)
6   Henry's employed in pleasant and highly appropriate position (5)
9   Caped crusader overcomes old bargee (7)
10 Row following hospital's volte-face becomes more unpleasant (7)
11 Records scores — they're put up on the wall (10)
12 Home care halved for ancient Indian (4)
14 Jacket father fastened round the chest (5)
15 Somewhat foolish and over the top (1,3,5)
16 Lackey has to pass on information in a specially prepared envelope (9)
18 Made authoritative statement with several lines (5)
20 Drop wrench (4)
21 Upset, is scared to get shunned (10)
25 Capital of Spain suffering setback after English became old (7)
26 Telling tales during confinement (5-2)
27 Standard or good score (5)
28 With time, a railway becomes less important (9)

DOWN

1   Prove wrong potato was picked up (5)
2   Run along quickly in small van (7)
3   Hazel's dependants put woolly jumpers over formal dress (5-5)
4   Imprisoned by king, I was a no-hoper (5)
5   This colour ain't green, strangely enough (9)
6   Informer is clued up, so to speak (4)
7   Letter expressing opposition to Italian wine (7)
8   Attention given to sheep set back by sheep-infesting parasite — it's set aside (9)
13 Appeal in pamphlet received by people lacking a leader (10)
14 Was perhaps performing neat steps (4,5)
15 I hid spasm, shaken to the core on board (9)
17 Copy, with time flying (7)
19 The French hit a snag — the dish is Italian (7)
22 Survivor from the past about to enjoy ice-cream cone shortly? (5)
23 Man about town welcomed by old and young (5)
24 Flower came up (4)

ACROSS

1 Shots heard — after drinking this? (8)
5 Setback for everyone in tragic city (6)
9 Painting's unfortunate feature, omitting one ring (8)
10 Disallow question posed by old Scottish general (6)
12 Morality play, one that uplifts absolutely all of us? (5,3,4)
15 False identity, one adopted by a girl, mostly (5)
16 Hurries back to coast, seeing spray (9)
18 Energy drug retired salesman brought in perforated container (6-3)
19 Thin food member rejected, consuming game (5)
20 Lively exchanges to share with bench, ultimately being taken into custody (3,3,6)
24 Exist essentially? Not out there! (6)
25 Like one who's lost tie and hasn't dressed (8)
26 Bags of pasta canteen finally disposed of (6)
27 Very large sign oddly covering part of Vietnam (8)

DOWN

1 Clan holding record in heartless self-interest (4)
2 Broadcast musical that may be electric! (4)
3 Self-seeker's call, one brought up in rare tizzy (9)
4 But it wasn't all easy going for the vicar of Wakefield (8,4)
6 A rook, possibly, crossing island at great speed (5)
7 Voluble crowd briefly cut charlatan over evidence of debts (10)
8 Standard work on farm, keeping first of sheep motionless (5-5)
11 Sourness of blokes with beer arrested by Met, perhaps (12)
13 Drink composer finally changed, putting on lid (10)
14 Bumped off and dumped outside resort (10)
17 Got inside, somehow, in process of breaking down (9)
21 Bottle opener vendors can provide (5)
22 Country fellow in Military Intelligence (4)
23 Speculator in a rut, perhaps? (4)

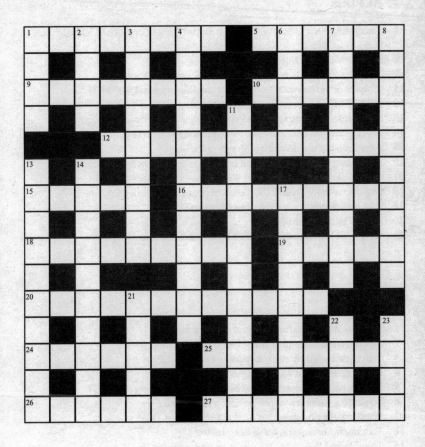

ACROSS

1 Decorating with utterly worthless material front of emporium and surround (12)
8 Doctor in choir out of lozenges (7)
9 Vehicle's bill for carrying football or cricket team about (7)
11 Chapter on love poetry essential for the Washington Post? (3,4)
12 Learn Bodleian periodically gets something on the Fleece (7)
13 Government department formerly eccentric and historically square (5)
14 Stirring around ten, quits Northern French town (2-7)
16 American nut's wild pogo with a beer (6,3)
19 In meeting places hard for one to find children's adventure writer (5)
21 Figures making a scene when not allowed to tour meadow (7)
23 Old character, with an exhortation to peer to return, displays spirit (7)
24 Had spin doctor turned over books, worried? (7)
25 Fail — as meters do (4,3)
26 New Irish PM upset with bank's high-risk behaviour (12)

DOWN

1 Work by Auden perhaps, a great piece of fiction (7)
2 Sky program that's infectious: one could get hooked! (7)
3 Mischievous fellow shifting purse or purses (7,2)
4 Bit of blooming pressure and rest is needed! (5)
5 Female managed opponents at bridge with neat intervention (7)
6 Something ornamental put on sink a hindrance (7)
7 Piano repairer holds up hat — one I should box (12)
10 Tucking into crackers, leave desserts (6,6)
15 Tremble and flee clutching grand, useless weapon (6,3)
17 One doing circuit judge's area is old (7)
18 Cannot reveal where this team hides up (7)
19 God's own judge carrying appeal skyward (7)
20 English corporal cuts short journey, finding a place to brood (7)
22 Let loose in French a curse, audibly (5)

ACROSS

1 Seen, heard, and put in one's place (5)
4 Burns, say, to cut chap out (9)
9 In court, no way cat's a god for Egyptian (9)
10 Study significance of green flower (5)
11 Use me around place, only on the outside (6)
12 Filled with depression, almost consumed by sloth (8)
14 As keyholder, very much dislike wonky nail in church (10)
16 Greet with small coin (4)
19 Engineer's cry of amazement some may pick up (4)
20 Some soldiers go potty about facial hair being trimmed (10)
22 The sign of the cross as a fertility symbol? (5,3)
23 Get some sleep on choice blanket (6)
26 Its operator turns needing coffee that's hot for a time (5)
27 People of capital settle our bill regularly in restaurants (9)
28 Decline to add two notes to closing phrase (9)
29 Travel regularly again, and come back (5)

DOWN

1 I'm safe from attack, having landed in barge (6,3)
2 In the end, political association is secure (3-2)
3 Regretted doddery old peer's died (8)
4 Commonly inflames worries (4)
5 A white man taking on domestic worker? No (10)
6 Put energy into inadequate triangular relationship (6)
7 In struggling men, Agnes inserting a component of steel (9)
8 Top person, or unimportant? (2,3)
13 Ranger finds a gull in lawned area (4,6)
15 Genuine article secured by Sally say as target reserve falls short (9)
17 Mine English awfully lousy, so attracting sympathy (9)
18 Harder to satisfy, finding nothing between chestnut and willow (8)
21 Finally, he goes for plan (6)
22 Some eels are said to be cold (5)
24 Huge speed on old car not doing much damage (5)
25 A priest and a bishop live together (4)

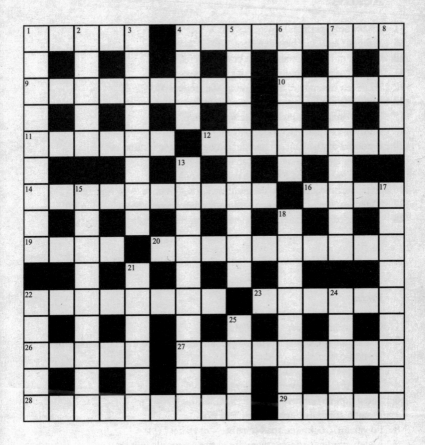

ACROSS

1   28 26 fools, perhaps? (8)
5   Time we have left between noon and midnight (6)
10 Clubbing, I'd be astounded to be this! (6,3,6)
11 Drop University student into open-air theatre (7)
12 Were any to change, this would be the time (3,4)
13 Auditor's not to overlook submarine? (8)
15 Love to acquire knowledge, being in range? (5)
18 European city district hard to avoid (5)
20 Producer of *Death Wish* had not sat out director's initial cut (8)
23 Loud outcry about the affair of 18 (7)
25 Happy and carefree loved one packs lacy pants (7)
26 Expect to succeed in trivial multiplication, but have to start again (4,2,6,3)
27 Sharp answer — difference, ultimately, between right and wrong (6)
28 Succeeded for West Ham, maybe, having Barnet under pressure? (8)

DOWN

1   Condescend to accept second plan (6)
2   One running the line has black eye, having received first of punches that hurt! (4-5)
3   SW runner on pleasing run (7)
4   Turn a screw, not even leaving mark (5)
6   Show how to improve short lives (4,3)
7   Woman going through Inkblot Test (5)
8   European's rocky old road to ruin — or riches? (8)
9   Lovely garden's so long there are various animals in it (8)
14 Most prominent in speed-dating at one talked-about joint, a ridiculous guy (8)
16 Like Salar the Salmon and Tarka the Otter — two animals, one with tail up (9)
17 I got depressed seven times writing this clue! (5,3)
19 One exceptional druggie (7)
21 Mischief-maker restricts almost all of movement that's slow in general (2,5)
22 At work, nurse's 1 *dn* (6)
24 Tie round the neck when lying on bed (5)
25 Frequent search over small area (5)

ACROSS

1 Assesses recruit involved in computer programs (9)
9 Weapon to get fixed again with extra power put in (7)
10 Monster caught a man having taken some time (7)
11 Pasta restricted, in short supply (5)
12 Overstate what may be made of smart idea (9)
13 A capital fellow needing a month for holidays, about (7)
15 Author's adversary, first person to change text around (5)
17 Feature of fabric of church in French street (5)
18 Inebriating litres downed by explosive female (5)
19 Elegant couple of characters finally returning after short ceremony (5)
20 Gift that is offered by publishing house (7)
23 Following a particular philosopher, Conservative as well (9)
25 Presenter of sporting trophy jockey's listened to (5)
27 Fresh bit of language in notes? No (7)
28 What garage door may be but not up in town (7)
29 Lamentations that could be shortened (9)

DOWN

1 Where you may find shops are invaded by bad man (6)
2 Demure ace with visage to enthral one initially before detailed examination (5,5)
3 Part of instrument surfacing in a river — there are tests here (8)
4 Crowd runs out to meet one religious teacher (5)
5 Gallery workers coming into street to issue bulletin (9)
6 Once saw agent clad in leather (6)
7 Itching that makes one cry (4)
8 Woman upsetting men, joining priests' institution having left home (8)
14 A thousand pounds — money very good coming in as funding for education? (5-2-3)
16 Force tour to get abandoned — vehicle may have pulled up here (9)
17 Final goodbye to one regarded as heretical at the bank (8)
18 Satellite's very energetic charged particle (8)
21 Struggled with stones on ramble (6)
22 Socialist sets undermining a printing unit (6)
24 One car about to join another for a spin (5)
26 Party after party? I'm dead! (4)

ACROSS

1 It digitally signals decision that could go either way (5)
4 Luggage taken from rear part forwards (9)
9 Primarily changeable in nature, perhaps (9)
10 Temperature, approximately, in part of body (5)
11 Family member finally taken home — what a relief! (6)
12 Fast pace disheartened famous person (8)
14 Left-winger covering point before being put on record (10)
16 At start of term, after job (4)
19 Bombed a long way away from base (4)
20 Benefit of rewriting centre page (10)
22 Significant evidence finally introduced in case by old lady (8)
23 Pound put in by person providing money for musician (6)
26 Constant pressure for bad sportsman (5)
27 Feature picture with parts people try to recall (9)
28 Little right to hold back as American, say (9)
29 Frenzied guy one follows with maximum possible speed (5)

DOWN

1 Turn to her at sea as guide for navigation (4,5)
2 Open University, new and better (5)
3 See Bruce, possibly, composing music for children (8)
4 Attend strike (4)
5 Conservative noncommittal about monarch in meeting (10)
6 Professional jargon of baker's man, for example? (6)
7 Carriage or van I arranged for cats, dogs, and others (9)
8 Ostentatious? Depends how you take part (5)
13 Information on energy helping production (10)
15 High achievers, those who understand Asians' game? (2-7)
17 After short time, dissenter welcomes old academic (9)
18 Obedient slave among those riding mare (5,3)
21 Show one's pain, putting horse in pen (6)
22 Bird originally mimicking a call of another (5)
24 This country invested in that part of North America (5)
25 Fruit repeatedly said to make couple trim (4)

This was the first qualifying puzzle for the 2010 Times Crossword Championship.

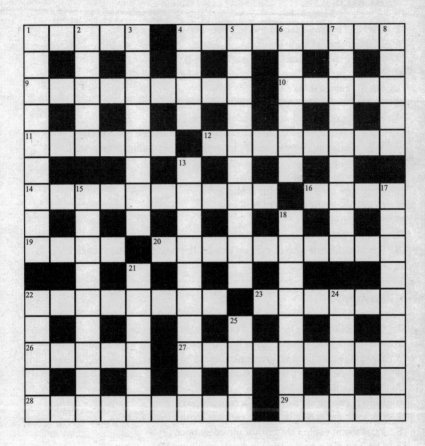

ACROSS

1 Poet and other writers producing Spoonerism books (9)
6 Discipline class (5)
9 PC equipment not hard to switch over (5-2)
10 Make privy to replace toilet round back of garden (3,4)
11 Small seabird is back (5)
12 Amid great euphoria, City makes recovery (9)
14 Teaching qualification — foundation level? (3)
15 Lack of feeling during jail term about inmates from the start (11)
17 Who'll arrange Algarve breaks in temporary accommodation? (6,5)
19 Slight wound (3)
20 Such females admitted to court? (9)
22 Language used in Kashmir is Hindi (5)
24 Got dressed and rode off (7)
26 A rebel at my school (7)
27 Son put tiny bit of money on lottery (5)
28 Spend too much time in gym on treadmill, principally, and shower later (9)

DOWN

1 One worshipped in Egypt, first out of large singing group (5)
2 We will stop newspaper editor making a bloomer (7)
3 Be sure one's raised severe displeasure? (4,5)
4 Cold venison served in dish becomes main focus of attention (6,5)
5 Not quite the only sun god (3)
6 Elderly person keeps books accessible (2,3)
7 Lothario appearing in formal garment, posh article (3,4)
8 Republican's sole vote cast for president once (9)
13 Don't be distracted — this is not the solution (11)
14 University fellows hog food? (4,5)
16 Plotter in Baltic city surrounded by explosive (9)
18 A banquet's starting with sole and shellfish (7)
19 Agree with artist's fanciful idea (7)
21 What implies students will be seen early in the day at Yale (5)
23 Obscure-sounding name for composer (5)
25 Two people united in celebration (3)

This was the second qualifying puzzle for the 2010 Times Crossword Championship.

ACROSS

1 Prize, of course, given after short party (8)
6 Drink fine vocalist endlessly required (6)
9 One who doesn't hang around drug dealer (5,8)
10 Large hole in case presented by barrister in conclusion (6)
11 Birdwatcher is in river in central France following goose (8)
13 Who'll help an Irish housewife clean up her mess? (10)
15 County cricket captain once facing over (4)
16 Get listener's reaction at the end (4)
18 Alley leads to Bow landmark? (6,4)
21 Contract to supply kiln written in specialised vocabulary (8)
22 He painted giant straddling island (6)
23 Went to rear of orchestra pit and played second fiddle? (4,1,4,4)
25 Carriage left one in European capital (6)
26 Trace element, cobalt, finally detected in preserve (8)

DOWN

2 Engage an understudy (7)
3 Get no bad distance, starting with a chemical spray (5,6)
4 Less than no place for looting (5)
5 Choose artist showing a complex character? (7)
6 Romantic partisan — leading article dropped for one (9)
7 American actor's riveting anecdotes (3)
8 Snooker player unknown in China, say (7)
12 Remark about district's bay (11)
14 Before noon, present oneself to commander over one's pardon (4,5)
17 Say, Judas's plot unravelled with endless ease (7)
19 Withdraw two-thirds of socialist pamphlet (7)
20 One making little effort to get beer mat (7)
22 Number pass inside producing voucher (5)
24 Hooter in arena leader's blown (3)

This was the third qualifying puzzle for the 2010 Times Crossword Championship.

ACROSS

1 A child will have to be mentioned (7,2)
6 Put down timetable, say, before the beginning of term (5)
9 General concluded with colleague briefly (7)
10 Reply with final message, circular letter set out (7)
11 In small piece allocated, leader of cellos played sweetly (5)
13 Some factory publications issued piecemeal (4,5)
14 Record to forget introducing deejay's first broadcast (9)
16 Move listlessly, but one circles the globe (4)
18 Rubbish dumped by a vale casually (2-2)
19 Agents settling for poor rates (9)
22 TV personality at hand before Queen appears (9)
24 Authority's spoken advice on how to pronounce "sew" (3-2)
25 Briskly demanding some equal leg-room (7)
26 Instrument in case, article at back of church (7)
28 Hands coming round had meal afterwards (5)
29 Attackers (not voluntary soldiers) of new military unit (4,5)

DOWN

1 Educationist, cross inside, was sulking (7)
2 Exclamation from 'ovel (3)
3 Stony bit over a yard covered in brown liquid (8)
4 Workers organised insolence in plant (5)
5 Bird in snare set up on hilltop? (9)
6 Dad with son getting fruit (6)
7 Study of ancient people reveals unexpected glory, so I say (11)
8 Gallows brought to premature end a male — for this? (7)
12 Suffer when allotment gets built on and go mad? (4,3,4)
15 Level debate, with clamour being kept outside (6,3)
17 Low-down character seen at the front of bars (4,4)
18 A pilot's sent out — one assists with movement of ship (7)
20 Keeping soldiers in field of action (7)
21 He may lead out bishop, having edge over rook (6)
23 Dances in party gowns when female comes out (5)
27 Time to leave prison for address befitting gentleman (3)

This was the fourth and last qualifying puzzle for the 2010 Times Crossword Championship.

ACROSS

1 Writer depicting manger in empty stable (6)
4 Hero's reformed party in Stormont given support (6,2)
9 Forestall result of execution? (4,3)
11 Keen to accept book shedding some light (7)
12 Two names for one in palace? (5)
13 Skilled hand and master at sea (9)
14 Characteristic of chef that divides New Zealanders (4,6)
16 Valiant person holding line (4)
19 Right here with name for Duke in song (4)
20 Seeing red drink smart chap has swallowed before it turned cold (10)
22 Tommy, often disheartened, is to persevere (7,2)
23 Outlaw backed by old bishop becomes a very wealthy man (5)
25 Musical instruction provided by an Italian poet (7)
26 Such a city is Rome, foreign but not unknown (7)
27 Male role in state occasion lacking men (3,5)
28 Girls, not first and second rate (6)

DOWN

1 I help cars turning round (9)
2 Willing to study close of play (5)
3 Illicit recording lacking finish seems extremely unprofitable (8)
5 Musical work a chef explains (4,1,8)
6 Stranger seen in glass (6)
7 Very attractive man possibly met aboard (9)
8 Don climbing down? (3,2)
10 Tense or terse utopian forecast (6,7)
15 Beau goes topless, having left port with too much on (9)
17 Egg producers avoid legislation (9)
18 Queen tucked into portion of pottage for spite (8)
21 Centre for financier, terribly naive about capital (6)
22 Drastically prune small and large tree (5)
24 Nut from the capital of Brazil, formerly (5)

This puzzle, used in the First Preliminary round of the 2010 Times Crossword Championship, was solved correctly within the time limit by 65% of the competitors.

ACROSS

1 After exam, a great place in life (8)
5 Shrewd-sounding Scots can't give battle (6)
9 Back in time, I am an egg (3)
10 Not self-conscious as one leaves for a desert here (11)
12 One used to glance as two fliers meet (7,3)
13 Area covered by wood is considerable (4)
15 Don't let go of contents of nest (6)
16 Joint presented in a way that didn't please (7)
18 Arid interior, blooming in the past (7)
20 Fairy — it is about to stop breathing (6)
23 After conflict, died in custody (4)
24 Incomer is a stranger in islands (10)
26 Artist's mother in law I cultivated, not the finished article (3,8)
27 Measure of warmth, though, evens out (3)
28 My bill goes down a bit, but debt collector gets nothing back (6)
29 Bob turns out to be refractory (8)

DOWN

1 Old republic is very pleasant around end of June (6)
2 Vicious criticism of musical group among numbers of Romans (7)
3 Hurls tree, showing beef (5,5)
4 Cheat Mack, and add a little sadism? (5,3,5)
6 Some yobs are up — to receive this? (4)
7 Trap with bouncer in game (7)
8 Where to get loaded, perhaps, stuffed with gold? (8)
11 Protection against whiplash started hernia off (4,9)
14 Orient footballers maybe used to exercise in the gym (6,4)
17 Employed to keep books, wife started probably illegally (3-5)
19 Do this with the towel perhaps that's taken off the field (5,2)
21 For fear, closing old house in the country (7)
22 Keep talking tediously? Exactly (4,2)
25 I party over island (4)

This puzzle, used in the First Preliminary round of the 2010 Times Crossword Championship, was solved correctly within the time limit by 38% of the competitors.

ACROSS

1   Complete a sort of clue that's spot on (9)
6   Virago novel about resistance shown by wife (5)
9   Music in traveller's lodge finally changed (5)
10 Is article crazy or sensible? (9)
11 Do language course before holiday, and depart unannounced (4,6,5)
13 PC's radio switched on and off (8)
14 Expert about to abandon craft (6)
16 Go down with disease when in trouble (6)
18 From entrance turned left regularly for church gallery (4,4)
21 It's why man with Greene novel is a writer (6,9)
23 Stand for troops here (9)
25 Girl from good book (5)
26 After short time it's clear he's a painter (5)
27 Secondary interests produce row between parties (9)

DOWN

1   Resign at half-time? (5)
2   How doors and drawers are made? Even more so (4,5,2)
3   Informer replacing criminals' leader takes the biscuit (7)
4   Evergreen from forest, one in a state (8)
5   Spell name — follow with one's finger round (6)
6   One offering slippery replies (7)
7   Work schedule left by a bunk (3)
8   Most wonderful bridge player holding deck I shuffled (9)
12 Misses running at end of relay race (11)
13 Caught with odd instrument in kitchen (5,4)
15 Trained to work? Made less as judge (8)
17 Start of play in, say, cricket test (7)
19 County where colleen's finished on top (7)
20 Women's stilettos in car (6)
22 Play's ending worries Irish writer (5)
24 Blast — the game's up (3)

This puzzle, used in the First Preliminary round of the 2010 Times Crossword Championship, was solved correctly within the time limit by 45% of the competitors.

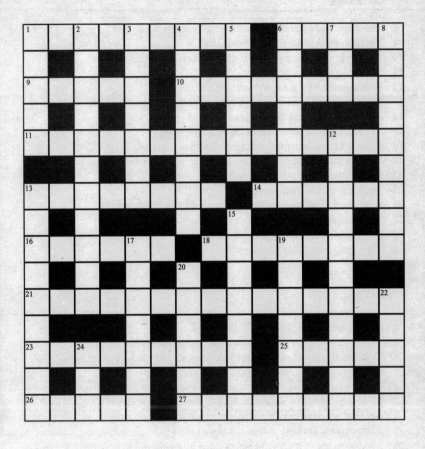

ACROSS

1 Prepare to leave hotel agent with a thousand on account (6)
4 Equip a cricket club like eccentrics (8)
10 Having trouble showing where the stock might end up (2,3,4)
11 Take delight in having friend, if down (3,2)
12 Bohemian family goes back on strike (7)
13 Disease killing last two in an advanced state, a severe blow (7)
14 Small group attracted to old instrument (5)
15 Spy receives clue when breaking atomic group (8)
18 What sounds like completely worthless pudding (4,4)
20 Shell's content, offering oil company fifty per cent of European capital (5)
23 Hall that's shabby but in good condition — bound to enter (7)
25 Summary of not totally impressive book (7)
26 Lyric prominent in every performance of Duke Ellington (5)
27 Step in glue, right in (9)
28 She's spun round and uses point (8)
29 Very lucky to engage new servant (6)

DOWN

1 Check clubs implicated in criminal break-in (4,4)
2 Difficulty with part of theatre season on Broadway (7)
3 Completely open land taken up for precision manufacturing area (5,4)
5 Robbery once provided dodgy dealer's wealth (7,7)
6 Plant hedging shrub, not the first on the edge (5)
7 Mishits ball badly, losing some length where grass grows (7)
8 Get through when East's ace is spread out (6)
9 Yank consortium built American skyscrapers (5,9)
16 Red colouring of meat joint surrounded by what's alight in barbecue? (9)
17 Hear about gibbons, perhaps the last in forest still hanging (8)
19 Romantic song's now disturbed rest (3,4)
21 Prevent from moving around to make sharper programme (5-2)
22 At a distance from a sphere (6)
24 Component that is incorporated in computer key (5)

*This puzzle, used in the Second Preliminary round of the 2010 Times Crossword
Championship, was solved correctly within the time limit by 40% of the competitors.*

Across

1   Luggage transporter's argument with bank (6)
4   Obscure surgeon breaking a verbal suspension of hostilities (8)
10 Crew leading unspecified number a merry dance! (9)
11 Northern oik's last drink taken outside low joint (5)
12 Remain calm, locks still being in place (4,4,4,2)
14 A Glaswegian, possibly, in Berkshire? (5)
16 Working in musical theatre, the writer's keeping time (9)
18 Protective covering of prime side when cooked (9)
20 Intolerant type shot during scrap (5)
21 Be good-humoured about fool's attractive role (4,2,4,4)
25 Farm pro executing volte-face in court (5)
26 Concerned with the office that ruined an Oxford college, say? (9)
27 Cash point replaced by chief — it requires a sovereign (8)
28 Languish aboard vessel (6)

Down

1   Mole's period of relaxation on river? (10)
2   Scoundrel casing university is received right away (5)
3   From distant settlement, published message on Internet (7)
5   It has branches in the Strand, do we hear? (5)
6   Extremely tedious song about end of Russian empress (7)
7   Lacking awareness, a Continental ruler accepts the present (9)
8   Woolly female Republican water-carrier (4)
9   Work Monet disguised, taking in American writer (4,4)
13 Favoured Irish town mostly hosting new athletic contest (10)
15 Mate with pull over quarter where Asians live (9)
17 Settle comfortably and study scene shot outside (8)
19 German prince raised duty, squeezing City traders at first (7)
20 Indulge in funnies, seeing item of camping gear! (7)
22 Bearing of brute regularly encountered in Japanese drama (5)
23 Copying silver-coated fastener (5)
24 Eccentric inferior to second fiddle (4)

This puzzle, used in the Second Preliminary round of the 2010 Times Crossword Championship, was solved correctly within the time limit by 63% of the competitors.

77

ACROSS

1   Be more tranquil and smooth-necked? (8)
5   Playwright about to perform as dog (6)
10 Burn up painting seized by rugby type (3,1,11)
11 Spoke about wild fen without restraint (10)
13 Blue material discovered in transmutation (4)
15 Tree in bed after tricky time? (7)
17 Cheese covering old church bread (7)
18 Wonderful rest is disturbed when everyone comes back in (7)
19 Mournful gale, swirling with ice (7)
21 Insensitive male breaking heart? (4)
22 End worked out with last of the pieces slotted in? (10)
25 Current effect of perceived bitterness (4,5,6)
27 Article involved in scandal, cut in perturbation (6)
28 Threefold work journey — short time reported (8)

DOWN

1   Baby food from room in contaminated area (7)
2   Development of one billion years (3)
3   Dead lifting apparatus for which one's sent off, possibly (4,6)
4   Millions buried in a remarkable battlefield (5)
6   Fool Henry beheaded to win round? (4)
7   What might have march menu I'd reprogrammed? (4,7)
8   Meteorological topic mostly covering start of rain and wind (7)
9   Echo as leaving rally? (8)
12 Don't overlook the writer's bloomer (6-2-3)
14 Forces PA to sneak off after absurd idea (4-2-4)
16 US has no borders after short revolution, Indian constituent's found (8)
18 Having strong cords function, tie the knot (7)
20 Nasty woman arrives with hot and cold symptom (7)
23 Sexy looker provides endless delight among men (5)
24 Spotty coverage in enclosure media finally put up (4)
26 Last ones in get no sherry trifle (3)

This puzzle, used in the Second Preliminary round of the 2010 Times Crossword Championship, was solved correctly within the time limit by 54% of the competitors.

ACROSS

1   Post **Lar**? (7)
5   Head over heels, desperate to wear finest stone (7)
9   Before the end of *Rigoletto*, bass part held back by great big noise (9)
10 Strike loudly, bearing lower (5)
11 Set off to catch man, clever, not a cheat (13)
13 Brave protagonist behind cape, eager to remain nameless (8)
15 Discomfort running, might this be? (6)
17 Jacket exposed at the front, assign pockets (6)
19 From here, drive anger out, a difficult issue? (8)
22 Prepared for battle, and striking? (7,2,4)
25 Sect ending in boxing ring (5)
26 Same agent arranged for Liberace, say (5,4)
27 Asian I'm sure put in the shade (7)
28 Conceive it, say, as something to bury (7)

DOWN

1   Fail to attack (4)
2   One was gifted, finding opening in shelter (7)
3   Party enters perfect defence (5)
4   Baby on the ball? (8)
5   Soft tripe that's to be disdained (6)
6   Amended appeal to round number, after partners secured by bishop (9)
7   Current man on board (7)
8   Ocean predator rights wrong, saving English ship (5,5)
12 Mouse minded to hide in tree, given no more time (7-3)
14 Slip open, inspiring whisper (9)
16 Memorial of Circe, not Aphrodite (8)
18 Young animal, born ram, we reared (3,4)
20 Giant curly thing in porker, twisted (7)
21 Inventor — one blasted off to orbit Pluto (6)
23 Take lid off vessel with temperature static (5)
24 One wing allowed to remain (4)

This puzzle, used in the Grand Final of the 2010 Times Crossword Championship, was solved correctly within the time limit by eight of the 24 competitors.

ACROSS

1 Tribute from group about saint connected with branch of medicine (9)
6 Question of vision with centre forward (5)
9 Expertise with storage of energy leading to jargon (5)
10 One can blame broadcast for bias (9)
11 Sound check (7)
12 Look at everything on yen harboured by revolutionary worker? (7)
13 Batting before break, entertaining play ignoring minute essentials of system (14)
17 Eminent figure's last rant seemed out of order (5,9)
21 Cheat in trouble in row (7)
23 Company around knight protecting religious conflict's location (7)
25 Financial aspects not at all grasped by jokers online? (9)
26 Lumber, no small muddle (5)
27 Urgency essential to triumph as team (5)
28 Group of trees cut by husband directly (5-4)

DOWN

1 Send payment, omitting nothing, to feed bird (8)
2 Shame to lack time for letter (5)
3 Reduce effect of uranium put away under trap army set up (9)
4 Term's record on tax, beginning to fall (7)
5 Frozen scene out around field (7)
6 Odd bits from litter lout, scattered material (5)
7 New in resort, quietly rising star (9)
8 Descendant of settlers from east inhabiting cold place (6)
14 Criminal use of lino in makeover (9)
15 Keen queen tucked into first piece of Turkish delight (9)
16 Ground we tend, OK for creeping plant (8)
18 Officer repeated phrase after woman (7)
19 Plaintiff having endless capital possessing advantage (7)
20 Hearts belonging to safe figurehead, quiet once more (6)
22 Feel good? Then stay, perhaps (5)
24 Stands to get help with work, given lift (5)

This puzzle, used in the Grand Final of the 2010 Times Crossword Championship, was solved correctly within the time limit by 18 of the 24 competitors.

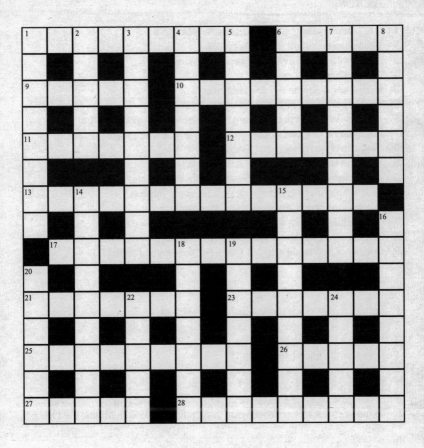

ACROSS

1 One's mum making this polite refusal, look (3,1,4)
5 Head chasing circuit for computer (6)
10 Needlewoman's embroidered lace — top drawer (9)
11 Girl married out of spite (5)
12 Hikes over moor, finally finding driver (4)
13 See intrigue when in a flap and weak (2,1,3,3)
15 Jack maybe hiding book — something Bob's often spotted (10)
17 Made charts of East London showing underground passage (4)
19 Come up close by source of Tweed? (4)
20 Kitchen worker lived with woman on dole (10)
22 After gymnastic stunts cheers very loudly, that's plain! (9)
24 Chap who's bright grasping one of three basic subjects? (4)
26 Is it not commonly Aussie can cut boomerangs? (5)
27 One shifting bristles with rage and coils up in defence (5,4)
28 Mark perhaps left by wound goes purple initially (6)
29 Outline of Shetland perhaps to the west, then second island (8)

DOWN

1 Scratch, cut or pinch form, whether good or bad (4)
2 Article to wear before ball, following college, and racing (3,5,2,5)
3 Report recalled dog swallowing gold band (3,5)
4 Divorcee turning pictures over (5)
6 French poet and topless model (6)
7 Rear people's children late, as I ordered (4-3,8)
8 Sister gathering a few bits in quarry for father's house (10)
9 Extreme characters are occupying unspecified position in Middle East town (8)
14 Pulling legs, pinch chap's bottom, naughtily (10)
16 Keen guards greeting lady, displaying it? (8)
18 Aussie skipper's bludgeoned 6 stopping decisive defeat (8)
21 Fly Trieste-Stansted after lifting bags (6)
23 Female for time in a panic, but not still (5)
25 Super being leader once crisis is over! (4)

This puzzle, used in the Grand Final of the 2010 Times Crossword Championship, was solved correctly within the time limit by 12 of the 24 competitors.

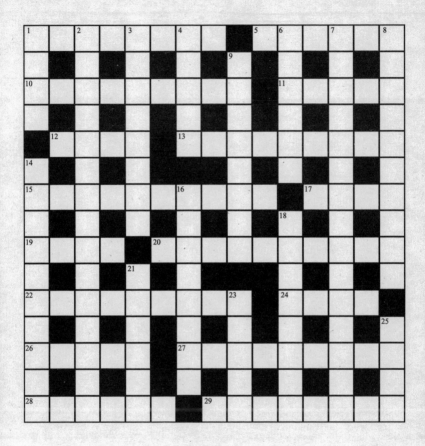

1

T	R	A	P		E	T	H	I	O	P	I	A	N	S
A		R		W		N		E		E		E		L
M	A	C	H	E	T	E		T	O	R	O	N	T	O
A		A		L		E		C		E		A		A
R	E	D	L	E	T	T	E	R		U	N	I	O	N
A		I		C		P		S		D		E		
C	H	A	R	T	E	R	H	O	U	S	E			
K		N		R		O		S		I		M		S
	F	O	R	T	H	E	M	O	M	E	N	T		
S		G		S		T		N		G		R		
A	W	A	I	T		E	N	C	H	I	L	A	D	A
M		R		A		N		A		S		P		I
S	T	A	R	T	E	R		P	U	T	D	O	W	N
O		G		I		O		E		D		E		
N	O	E	L	C	O	W	A	R	D		B	E	A	D

2

B	E	A	N	B	A	G		T	O	N	I	G	H	T
O		C		E		A		A		U		L		R
S	E	Q	U	E	S	T	E	R	E	D		A	N	A
T		U		K		E		A		G		Z		V
O	L	I	V	E	R		A	D	H	E	S	I	V	E
N		R		E		M		I		E		E		R
	E	S	P	R	I	T	D	E	C	O	R	P	S	
B		E		C		D		H						E
U	N	D	E	R	W	H	E	L	M	I	N	G		
T		R		A		E		P		U		H		
T	E	E	N	A	G	E	R		M	O	R	A	L	E
R		A		P		L		A		L		N		R
E	L	M		P	O	M	E	G	R	A	N	A	T	E
S		E		A		E		T		C		O		
S	E	R	I	O	U	S		D	R	A	G	O	O	N

3

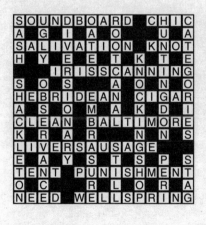

4

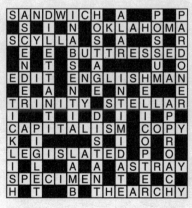

SOLUTIONS

5

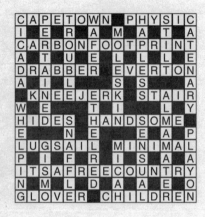

```
C A P E T O W N   P H Y S I C
I   E   R   A   M   A   T   A
C A R B O N F O O T P R I N T
A   T   U   E   L   L   L   E
D R A B B E R   E V E R T O N
A   I   L   S   S   S   A   A
  K N E E J E R K   S T A I R
W   E   T   I   L   Y
H I D E S   H A N D S O M E
E   N   E   E   A   P
L U G S A I L   M I N I M A L
P   I   F   R   I   S   A   A
I T S A F R E E C O U N T R Y
N   M   L   D   A   A   E   O
G L O V E R   C H I L D R E N
```

6

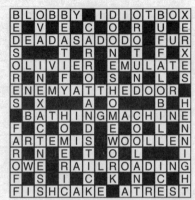

```
B L O B B Y   I D I O T B O X
E   V   E   C   O   R   U   E
D E A D A S A D O D O   F U R
S     T   R   N   T   F   X
O L I V I E R   E M U L A T E
R   N   F   O   S   N   L   S
E N E M Y A T T H E D O O R
S   X     A   O   B   H
  B A T H I N G M A C H I N E
F   C   O   D   E   O   L   N
A R T E M I S   W O O L L E N
R   N   E   T   O   L     I
O W E   R A I L R O A D I N G
F   S   I   C   K   N   C   H
F I S H C A K E   A T R E S T
```

7

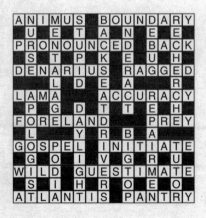

```
A N I M U S   B O U N D A R Y
  U   E   T   A   N   E   E
P R O N O U N C E D   B A C K
  S   T   P   K   E   U   H
D E N A R I U S   R A G G E D
  L   D   E   A   R
L A M A   A C C U R A C Y
  P   G   D   T   T   E   H
F O R E L A N D   P R E Y
  L   Y   R   B   A
G O S P E L   I N I T I A T E
  G   O   I   V   G   R   U
W I L D   G U E S T I M A T E
  S   I   H   R   O   E   O
A T L A N T I S   P A N T R Y
```

8

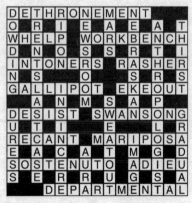

```
D E T H R O N E M E N T
O   R   I   E   A   E   A   T
W H E L P   W O R K B E N C H
D   N   O   S   S   R   T   I
I N T O N E R S   R A S H E R
N   S     O     S   R   S
G A L L I P O T   E K E O U T
    A   N   M   S   A   P
D E S I S T   S W A N S O N G
U   T   I     E     L   R
R E C A N T   M A R I P O S A
E   A   C   A   T   M   G   D
S O S T E N U T O   A D I E U
S   E   R   R   U   G   S   A
    D E P A R T M E N T A L
```

9

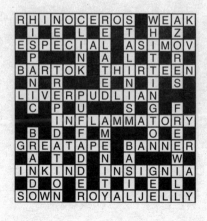

```
F A R T H E R ■ B E G G A R ■
O ■ E ■ A ■ E ■ E ■ O ■ V ■
R E S T R A I N T ■ I R I S H
T ■ E ■ R ■ N ■ R ■ N ■ A ■ O
H A R D Y ■ S L A U G H T E R
E ■ V ■ ■ U ■ Y ■ O ■ O ■ S
P I E C H A R T ■ A V E R S E
R ■ ■ A ■ E ■ E ■ E ■ ■ S
E N D I N G ■ A P P R O A C H
S ■ I ■ D ■ A ■ I ■ ■ Q ■ O
E N V I S A G E D ■ D E U C E
N ■ E ■ D ■ H ■ E ■ E ■ A ■ C
T O R S O ■ A L M A M A T E R
■ G ■ W ■ S ■ I ■ U ■ I ■ A
■ P E A N U T ■ C O R N C O B
```

10

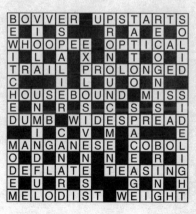

```
S U N K I S S E D ■ R O S E S
H ■ A ■ N ■ L ■ I ■ A ■ T ■ T
A P I N G ■ I N S T I G A T E
M ■ L ■ L ■ C ■ T ■ T ■ B ■ A
B E S P E A K ■ A V A I L E D
L ■ ■ N ■ L ■ F ■ ■ E ■ Y
E C O N O M Y O F S C A L E ■
S ■ D ■ O ■ ■ ■ O ■ A ■ H
■ P A C K A G E H O L I D A Y
M ■ L ■ ■ A ■ E ■ L ■ ■ D
O M I N O U S ■ L E A N D E R
R ■ S ■ N ■ P ■ L ■ P ■ R ■ O
R E Q U I S I T E ■ S W I N G
I ■ U ■ C ■ N ■ N ■ E ■ L ■ E
S I E G E ■ G W E N D O L E N
```

11

```
R H I N O C E R O S ■ W E A K
■ I ■ E ■ L ■ E ■ T ■ H ■ Z
E S P E C I A L ■ A S I M O V
■ P ■ ■ N ■ A ■ L ■ T ■ R
B A R T O K ■ T H I R T E E N
N ■ R ■ ■ E ■ N ■ I ■ S
L I V E R P U D L I A N ■ ■
■ C ■ P ■ U ■ ■ S ■ G ■ F
■ ■ I N F L A M M A T O R Y
■ B ■ D ■ F ■ M ■ ■ O ■ E
G R E A T A P E ■ B A N N E R
■ A ■ T ■ D ■ N ■ A ■ ■ W
I N K I N D ■ I N S I G N I A
■ D ■ O ■ E ■ T ■ I ■ E ■ L
S O W N ■ R O Y A L J E L L Y
```

12

```
B O V V E R ■ U P S T A R T S
E ■ I ■ S ■ ■ R ■ A ■ E ■ O
W H O O P E E ■ O P T I C A L
I ■ L ■ A ■ X ■ N ■ T ■ O ■ I
T R A I L ■ P R O L O N G E D
C ■ ■ I ■ L ■ U ■ O ■ N ■
H O U S E B O U N D ■ M I S S
E ■ N ■ R ■ S ■ C ■ S ■ S ■ I
D U M B ■ W I D E S P R E A D
■ I ■ C ■ V ■ M ■ A ■ ■ E
M A N G A N E S E ■ C O B O L
O ■ D ■ N ■ N ■ E ■ R ■ ■ I
D E F L A T E ■ T E A S I N G
E ■ U ■ R ■ S ■ ■ G ■ N ■ H
M E L O D I S T ■ W E I G H T
```

SOLUTIONS

13

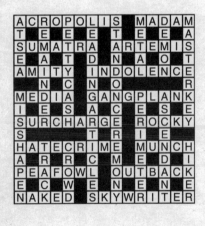

SANCTION GOWEST
AQUA ATTRACTIVE
HITTHEROAD HINT
OSOLEMIO UNRIPE
JEEVES FIELDING
EWER HERETOFORE
EFFORTLESS CREW
VESSEL REYNOLDS

14

HARDLEFT BYPASS
NOD DINNERLADY
OLIVEOYL ALEXIS
CLOG DARWINISTS
BUTTERMILK KALI
ATRIUM KOWTOWED
REDCABBAGE REV
TRIFLE PREDATOR

15

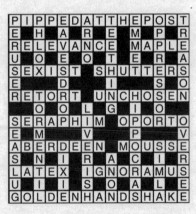

ACROPOLIS MADAM
SUMATRA ARTEMIS
AMITY INDOLENCE
MEDIA GANGPLANK
SURCHARGE ROCKY
HATECRIME MUNCH
PEAFOWL OUTBACK
NAKED SKYWRITER

16

PIPPEDATTHEPOST
RELEVANCE MAPLE
SEXIST SHUTTERS
RETORT UNCHOSEN
SERAPHIM OPORTO
ABERDEEN MOUSSE
LATEX IGNORAMUS
GOLDENHANDSHAKE

17

M	A	I	N	C	L	A	U	S	E		O	P	A	L
M		A		S		O		L		U		A		E
C	H	A	I	N	U	P		M	A	J	O	R	C	A
E		D		S		I		M		U		T		T
	P	O	R	T	E	N	T	O	U	S		N	O	H
S		R		E		E		N		T		E		E
C	H	A	I	R	S		V	E	N	T	U	R	E	R
A		N		P		R		H						I
P	O	P	P	A	D	U	M		S	E	X	T	O	N
E		O		T		N		U		T		E		G
G	Y	M		I	N	C	E	N	D	I	A	R	Y	
O		F		O		H		W		C		R		A
A	R	R	A	N	G	E		I	N	K	L	I	N	G
T		E		O		S		E		E		E		E
S	I	T	E		U	N	R	E	S	T	O	R	E	D

18

T	U	G	O	F	W	A	R		L		M		H
N		B		R		E	T	E	R	N	I	T	Y
L	I	V	E		A		P		G		N		P
C		R	E	P	E	R	C	U	S	S	I	O	N
Y		A		I		M		P		P			O
S	C	A	M	P	I		S	P	E	C	I	O	U	S
	L		M		N		E			C			I
R	E	V	E	N	G	E		J	A	C	K	A	S	S
E		R		S		M		A		H				
D	O	G	G	E	R	E	L		B	A	N	T	A	M
G		A		E		A		R		D		M		
I	N	A	U	S	P	I	C	I	O	U	S		B
A		C		E		K		S			P	I	L	L
N	O	M	I	N	A	T	E		I		A		E
T		E		T		N	E	A	T	N	E	S	S

19

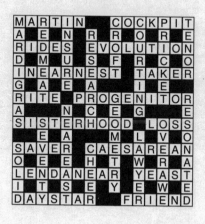

M	A	R	T	I	N		C	O	C	K	P	I	T
A		E		N		R		R	O	R		E	
R	I	D	E	S		E	V	O	L	U	T	I	O	N
D		M		U		S		F		R		C		O
I	N	E	A	R	N	E	S	T		T	A	K	E	R
G		A		E		A			I		E			
R	I	T	E		P	R	O	G	E	N	I	T	O	R
A			N		C		E		G					E
S	I	S	T	E	R	H	O	O	D		L	O	S	S
		E		A			M		L		V		O	
S	A	V	E	R		C	A	E	S	A	R	E	A	N
O		E		H		T		W		R		A		
L	E	N	D	A	N	E	A	R		Y	E	A	S	T
I		T		S		E		Y		E		W		E
D	A	Y	S	T	A	R		F	R	I	E	N	D

20

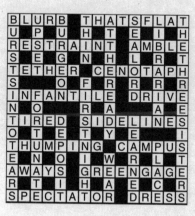

B	L	U	R	B		T	H	A	T	S	F	L	A	T
U		P		U		H		T		E		I		H
R	E	S	T	R	A	I	N	T		A	M	B	L	E
S		E		G		N		H		L		R		T
T	E	T	H	E	R		C	E	N	O	T	A	P	H
S			O		F		R		R		R		R	
I	N	F	A	N	T	I	L	E		D	R	I	V	E
N		O		R			A			A		A		E
T	I	R	E	D		S	I	D	E	L	I	N	E	S
O		T		E		T		Y		E			I	
T	H	U	M	P	I	N	G		C	A	M	P	U	S
E		N		O		I		W		R		L		T
A	W	A	Y	S		G	R	E	E	N	G	A	G	E
R		T		I		H		A		E		C		R
S	P	E	C	T	A	T	O	R		D	R	E	S	S

SOLUTIONS

21

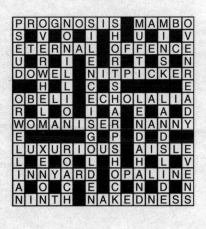

22

```
C A F F   H O W D O Y O U D O
  P O A   E U     S   N
S P O R T S C A S T   C A B S
  L   A B   T   W   G   E
T I N G L E   H E A D R E S T
  C   E E   E S       I
M A R C   N O R T H E R N E R
  T   A     F     A   R
H I P P O D R O M E   N E R D
  O     I   R   C   G   A
S N O W H O L E   O N E I L L
W   M     C   C   N   L   E
O M E N   E L A B O R A T O R
O   G     S   S   M   N   N
P L A N G E N T L Y   D Y E R
```

23

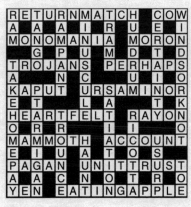

24

```
R E T U R N M A T C H   C O W
A A   A   I   R   U E   I
M O N O M A N I A   M O R O N
  G   P   U   M   D   T   D
T R O J A N S   P E R H A P S
A     N   C     U   I     O
K A P U T   U R S A M I N O R
E   T     L   A     T   K
H E A R T F E L T   R A Y O N
O   R   R     I   I       O
M A M M O T H   A C C O U N T
E   I   U   A   T   O S
P A G A N   U N I T T R U S T
A   A   C   N   O T   R   O
Y E N   E A T I N G A P P L E
```

25

```
H O A X E D   G O O D Y B A G
Y   R   L   N   R   R   A   I
P A C K A G I N G   I B S E N
E   A   L   N   A   F   S   G
R E D T A P E   N I T P I C K
I   I   M   D   I       S   O
O S A G E   A E S T H E T E
N   I   Y   E   O       M
  A G O N I S E D   P A S H A
M   E   W   C   S   A   N
I O N E S C O   R E C O U N T
S   T   P   N   I   O   C   I
S K I R L   D E M E T R I U S
U   L   I   E   E   C   E   S
S E E S T A R S   S H A R I A
```

26

```
P I C K L E D   F I T N E S S
U   A   O   E   O   E   L   W
F I R E W A T E R   Q U A K E
F   T   D   E   U   N   N   A
I R O K O   R E M A I N D E R
N   U   W   M   L       N   I
  C O N S I D E R A T I O N
I   H   N   X   N       G
S W E E T T E M P E R E D
L   O   A   E   U   B
A U T O M A T O N   D E C O R
M   O   B   E   S   U   T   I
I G L O O   S T I T C H I N G
S   E   L   T   V   E   H
E S T U A R Y   E A R N E S T
```

27

```
R A M S H A C K L E   A Y A H
I   A   I   E   P   R   R   R
C O N V E R S E   O G R E S S
E   T   T   P   N   I   E
P O R T   I N A N Y E V E N T
A   A   G   L   M   I   A
P U P P Y H O O D   P S A L M
E   R   T   W   H   T   A
R A V E N   O P T O M E T R Y
  R   D   B   R   U   E   B
C A D A V E R O U S   I S L E
  M   T   L   F   E   S   E
W A P I T I   I N D O L E N T
  I   O   E   L   O   R   L
S C A N   F R E I G H T A G E
```

28

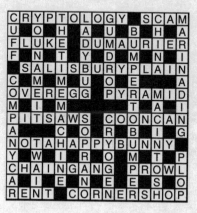

```
C R Y P T O L O G Y   S C A M
U   O   H   A   U   B   H   A
F L U K E   D U M A U R I E R
F   N   T   Y   D   M   N   I
  S A L I S B U R Y P L A I N
C   M   M   U   O   E   A
O V E R E G G   P Y R A M I D
M   I   M       T   A   I
P I T S A W S   C O O N C A N
A   C   O   R   B   I   G
N O T A H A P P Y B U N N Y
Y   W   I   R   O   M   T   P
C H A I N G A N G   P R O W L
A   I   E   N   E   E   S   O
R E N T   C O R N E R S H O P
```

SOLUTIONS

29

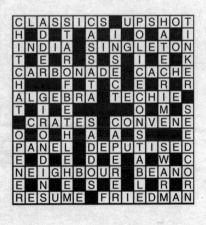

30

```
H I D E   A F I C I O N A D O
O   I     I   A U V   V
L U C I F E R   C A T H O D E
U   T O S   A   D   C   R
S C A R L E T T O H A R A
B   T   I P   M   D   S
O X E Y E   O U T A N D O U T
L   S S   A   E     A
U L A N B A T O R   D R O I T
S   U E     P S M   U
    C A R D I N A L P O I N T
G   T G D   U O C E
N A I V E T E   L A T E R A L
A   O R   A I     O A
W O N D E R L A N D   S N O W
```

31

32

```
H E L L F O R L E A T H E R
O   A   R O G W N   T
L I T T E R B U G   E A T E R
D   I S   U N N   I   A
O O M P H   S H O R T S T O P
N   E     T G Y L D
E A R L G R E Y   B O L E R O
S     R R P N     O
H O O D O O   J E W E L L E R
O   L U S T     E   S
R E D I N G O T E   C H A M P
S   G D   V R O   R   I
E D I T H   I L L O M E N E D
S   R O E E   B E   E
  F L I G H T R E C O R D E R
```

33

```
B U T T R E S S   M A S S I F
E   I   E   O       N   O   A
C O M P L I C I T   T A L O N
A   O   E   I   O   I   I   C
M O N T A N A   N I G H T L Y
E       S   L   G   U   A   I
    P R E O C C U P A T I O N
S   O       H       E   R   G
W H I T E H A R T L A N E
A   N   V   P   W   V       U
P A T R I O T   I S O S P I N
P   L   D   E   S   C   R   I
I M A G E   R I T U A L I S T
N   C   N       E   D   O   E
G R E E T S   A R M O U R E D
```

34

```
O B E R O N   P A D D L I N G
  A   A   I   H   O   O   A
U S E F U L L Y   N U B B I N
  R   F   L   K   S   L
C E L L O P H A N E   T A S K
  L   E   A       Y   E
P I U S   M E A N D E R I N G
  E       P   P   E       I
A F R I C A S T A R   C I T E
  N   S       B   O   P
U T A H   G R A V Y T R A I N
  O   U   R   M   P   C
C R I M E A   M O U S S A K A
  S   A   S   A   S   E   E
G O I N G S O N   E N D U R E
```

35

```
S O F I A   M A R T I N M A S
H   I   S   A   E   N   A   O
O V E R S L E E P   I D I O M
W   I   L   R   T   D   E
J U S T S O S T O R I E S
U   L   T   T   A   E   W
M E A N   D R A M A T U R G E
P   U   A   O   E   E   V   I
E N G A G E M E N T   C A L M
R   H   G       S   C   N   A
    T A R K A T H E O T T E R
A   E   I   L   E   U   A
M E R L E   L I V E R Y M A N
A   E   V   O   I   S   O   E
H O R S E B A C K   E N T E R
```

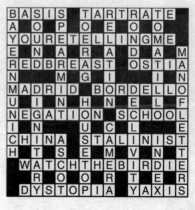

36

```
B A S I S   T A R T R A T E
A   O   P   O   E   O   O
Y O U R E T E L L I N G M E
E   N   A   R   A   D   A   M
R E D B R E A S T   O S T I A
N   M   G   I       I   N
M A D R I D   B O R D E L L O
U   I   N   H   N   E   L   F
N E G A T I O N   S C H O O L
I   N       U   C   L       E
C H I N A   S T A L I N I S T
H   T   S   E   M   V   N   T
  W A T C H T H E B I R D I E
    R   O   O   R   T   E   R
  D Y S T O P I A   Y A X I S
```

SOLUTIONS

37

```
A R T I C H O K E   T O P I C
N   A   H   U   F   A   I   O
V A L I A N T   T E R R A I N
I   L   L   O   O   N   C
L A B E L   F R O S T B I T E
    O   E   T   B   S   I
B A Y   N I H I L O B S T A T
A   G   E   I   A   E
T O I L E T W A T E R   R O D
H   M   A   E   M   E
T O M S A W Y E R   A S P I C
O   O   G   A   G   R   A
W A R L O C K   T A N D O O R
E   A   N   I   E   E   O E
L U L L Y   D O D U T Y F O R
```

38

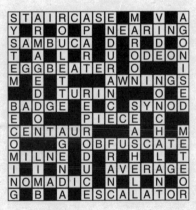

```
S U B S I D I A R Y   G R I T
I   E   N   N   U   A   O
R E L O C A T I N G   T I N Y
E   A   A   U   S   W   L   S
  S T O R M I N A T E A C U P
S   E   C   T   W   D   A   A
T I D I E R   M A N D A R I N
A   R   R   G   Y   I   I
L A C K A D A Y   E N T R E E
W   R   T   L   G   G   A   L
A N I D E A L H U S B A N D
R   M   D   I   N   E   S   M
T O S H   C A N N E L L O N I
L   O   R   E   L   M   S
Y A N K   A D O L E S C E N T
```

39

```
N I C K   B R A N D I S H E D
O   A   C   E   I   M   A   R
M A N H A N D L E   P A R K A
I   O   M   E   C   A   M   W
N A N K E E N   E U S T O N
A   R   S   S   N   I
T A S M A N I A N D E V I L S
I   Q   G   E   C   O
V A U G H A N W I L L I A M S
E   A   A   G   A   E
  T W I L I T   H O U D I N I
D   K   C   E   B   R   N   S
E D I F Y   H O O V E R D A M
A   N   O   E   U   L   I   A
L O G A N B E R R Y   M A I L
```

40

```
S T A I R C A S E   M   V   A
Y   R   O   P   N E A R I N G
S A M B U C A   D   R   D   O
T   A   L   R   U   O D E O N
E G G B E A T E R   O   I
M   E   T   A W N I N G S
  D   T U R I N   O   E
B A D G E   E C   S Y N O D
E   O   P I E C E   C
C E N T A U R   A   H   M
O   G   O B F U S C A T E
M I L N E   D   R   H   L   T
I   I   N   U   A V E R A G E
N O M A D I C   N   L   N   O
G   B   A   E S C A L A T O R
```

41

```
V I N E G A R I S H   S L I P
O   O   R   A   H   Y   A   U
C O N C E I T   O B O I S T S
A   E   E   E   T   R   S   S
L O V I N G C U P   K O O K Y
    E   H   A   U   S       F
K I N D A   P I T C H I N T O
I   T   M       I   E   O
L O S E C O U N T   R O O S T
O   O   N   W   E   L
H O K U M   C H I L D H O O D
E   E   M   L   N   A   G   I
R A N S O M E   B A L D I N G
T   D   N   A   E   E   S   I
Z O O M   I R I D E S C E N T
```

42

```
P R O F I T   R A B E L A I S
  O   L   O   O   U   U   N
J U R Y R I G G E D   C O D A
  N   W   L   E   D   I   O
A D H E R E N T   H I D I N G
    I   D   S   I       E
F R O G   T A S T I E S T
  O   H   F   H   T   N   I
S U I T C A S E       C H A T
  T   T   S   R   E
K I T S C H   A V E R S I V E
  N   O   O   U   M   S   O
V I E W   M A R G I N A L I A
  S   E   E   U   S   N   L
H E B R I D E S   S A T R A P
```

43

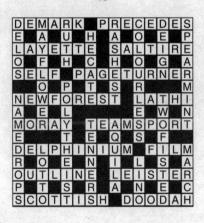

44

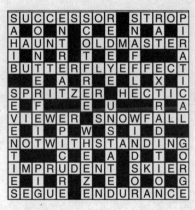

SOLUTIONS

45

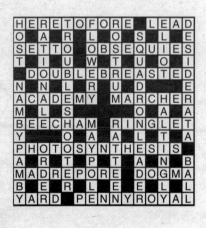

46

```
FEWEST OBSCURED
A  R  T   F E  A   A   A  E
TRAVELLER  REBUS
I  N  E   I K  T   I   E
MUG ROGUETRADER
A  L   H L   L   I   T
 REPORT ENDORSE
P  R  U S  Y  G   E   R
ROSETTE STEADY
E   W R  Q   M  T
SITTINGDUCK USE
E  R  T E  A  A  L  A
ROUGH ACROPOLIS
V  C  I N  E  U  E  E
EDENTATE STATER
```

47

48

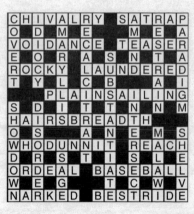

49

```
R I C H T E R   H O T S H O T
E   E   E   A   I   H   O   A
B A N K M A N A G E R   L I P
U   T   P   D   H   E   I   E
F L A G O N   F L A W L E S S
F   U   R   D   I   S   T
    R E A D I N G M A T T E R
B     R   S   H   P     Y
R U G B Y F O O T B A L L
E   E     R   S   R   E   F
A N T I B O D Y   O T T A W A
T   A   A   E   P   H   F   C
H E W   S E R V I C E F L A T
E   A   I   L   S   I   E   O
R O Y A L T Y   A U D I T O R
```

50

```
O F F I C I A L   P H O E B E
R   O   O   N   I   F   L   L
A I R H O S T E S S   S K E W
C   T   K   O   T   O   S
L E W I S A N D H A R R I S
E   O   O   Y   C   T   M
S U R I N A M   W H I S P E R
    T   R       I   L
S C H M U C K   S O P R A N O
    A   O   T   U   E   Y   R
P U B L I C S P I R I T E D
    T   C   R   I   H   E
B I L L   F R I E N D L I E R
O   E   O   M   O   N   L
U N I S E X   C O T T A G E Y
```

51

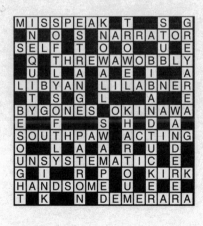

52

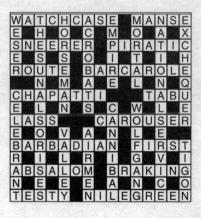

SOLUTIONS

53

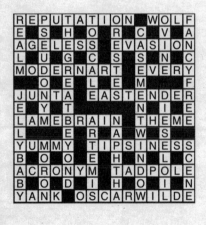

M	E	T	T	E	R	N	I	C	H		U	R	G	E
	X	I		A		N		O	N		A			
R	E	S	E	R	V	E	D		T	A	T	A	M	I
	C			E		E		B		O	B			
M	U	S	L	I	N		P	L	U	G	U	G	L	Y
	T		I			T		T	C		E			
D	O	W	N	T	H	E	H	A	T	C	H			
	R		E		U			O	A	P				
		D	I	N	G	D	O	N	G	B	E	L	L	
	S		A		C		E			L	O			
W	H	I	N	C	H	A	T		B	R	E	A	S	T
	E		C		B		R		O		I			
P	A	T	I	N	A		A	B	L	A	T	I	V	E
	T			C		I	U		A	E				
S	H	A	G		K	I	N	G	S	C	R	O	S	S

54

D	R	E	A	M	U	P		R	O	C	K	A	L	L
A		X		Y		I	E		R		R		E	
N	U	T		F	A	L	S	E	B	O	T	T	O	M
D		R	O		E		D		C		O			
A	N	A	C	O	N	D	A		T	U	C	S	O	N
R		V		T		R	R		S		E		D	
E	O	I	N		P	I	C	A	R	E	S	Q	U	E
	R		I	V		Z		S		U				
W	A	G	E	F	R	E	E	Z	E		W	E	L	L
H		I		F		R	M		D	S		S	U	
A	U	N	T	I	E		M	A	J	E	S	T	I	C
T			N	U	T		M		T	M		R	K	
N	U	M	B	E	R	P	L	A	T	E		A	D	O
O		O	S	T		Z		A	T	U				
T	A	B	A	S	C	O		Z	A	N	I	E	S	T

55

R	E	P	U	T	A	T	I	O	N		W	O	L	F
E		S		H		O		R	C		V		A	
A	G	E	L	E	S	S		E	V	A	S	I	O	N
L		U	G	C		S		S	N		C			
M	O	D	E	R	N	A	R	T		E	V	E	R	Y
	O	E		L	E		M				F			
J	U	N	T	A		E	A	S	T	E	N	D	E	R
E		Y	T			N		I		E				
L	A	M	E	B	R	A	I	N		T	H	E	M	E
L			E	R	A	W		S						
Y	U	M	M	Y		T	I	P	S	I	N	E	S	S
B		O	O	E		H		N	L		C			
A	C	R	O	N	Y	M		T	A	D	P	O	L	E
B		O	D	I		H		O	I		N			
Y	A	N	K		O	S	C	A	R	W	I	L	D	E

56

C	O	N	V	E	R	G	E		C	R	E	D	I	T
A		O		R		R		O		R			R	
A	T	E	R	R	I	F	I	E	R		M	I	A	M	I
H		M		T		N		E		A		M	M	
A	U	S	T	R	I	A		M	A	N	M	A	D	E
R		E		N		O		S		T		T		
		B	O	A	R	D	I	N	G	H	O	U	S	E
C	O			B		S			R			R		
O	N	A	S	H	O	E	S	T	R	I	N	G		
O		T		I		A		R		M				S
P	A	R	A	D	O	R		A	S	P	H	A	L	T
E		A		I		T		E		M			R	
D	U	C	A	L		T	H	I	R	T	Y	O	N	E
U		E		G			O		U		U		A	
P	A	S	T	O	R		A	N	G	S	T	R	O	M

184

57

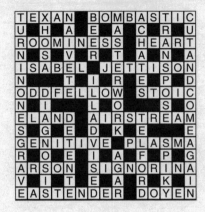

```
T E X A N ■ B O M B A S T I C
U ■ H ■ A ■ E ■ A ■ C ■ R ■ U
R O O M I N E S S ■ H E A R T
N ■ S ■ V ■ R ■ T ■ A ■ N ■ A
I S A B E L ■ J E T T I S O N
N ■ ■ ■ T ■ I ■ R ■ E ■ P ■ D
O D D F E L L O W ■ S T O I C
N ■ I ■ L ■ O ■ ■ ■ S ■ O ■ ■
E L A N D ■ A I R S T R E A M
S ■ G ■ E ■ D ■ K ■ E ■ ■ ■ E
G E N I T I V E ■ P L A S M A
R ■ O ■ E ■ I ■ A ■ F ■ P ■ G
A R S O N ■ S I G N O R I N A
V ■ I ■ T ■ E ■ A ■ R ■ K ■ I
E A S T E N D E R ■ D O Y E N
```

58

```
M Y C O S I S ■ S A T A N I C
O ■ A ■ T ■ P ■ E ■ R ■ O ■ O
V O L A U V E N T ■ U N M A N
E ■ O ■ N ■ C ■ S ■ C ■ I ■ J
■ M A G N I L O Q U E N C E ■
I ■ E ■ M ■ N ■ L ■ A ■ C ■ ■
M A L A D I E S ■ M E R L O T
P ■ ■ ■ E ■ N ■ C ■ N ■ ■ ■ U
O P T I C S ■ P O T T E R E R
R ■ E ■ R ■ C ■ V ■ ■ ■ I ■ E
T E N D E R H E A R T E D ■ ■
A ■ S ■ M ■ I ■ L ■ R ■ E ■ L
N O E L E ■ P H E R O M O N E
C ■ U ■ N ■ P ■ N ■ L ■ U ■ V
E M P A T H Y ■ T O L S T O Y
```

59

```
H Y D E ■ W I N D O W S E A T
E ■ A ■ ■ ■ S ■ O ■ O ■ L ■ W
L A M B A D A ■ U P R A I S E
I ■ N ■ U ■ A ■ B ■ D ■ C ■ N
P R A C T I C A L ■ P R I N T
A ■ B ■ O ■ ■ ■ E ■ R ■ T ■ Y
D E L I B E R A T I O N ■ ■ ■
S ■ E ■ I ■ A ■ O ■ C ■ A ■ C
■ ■ C O M M O N W E A L T H
P ■ A ■ G ■ R ■ ■ ■ S ■ P ■ A
L A S E R ■ A D M I S S I O N
A ■ S ■ A ■ I ■ E ■ O ■ N ■ C
C H I P P E D ■ D O R M I C E
I ■ S ■ H ■ E ■ E ■ ■ ■ S ■ R
D A I L Y B R E A D ■ S T A Y
```

60

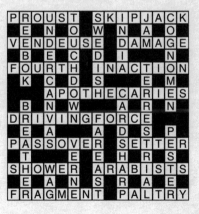

```
P R O U S T ■ S K I P J A C K
■ E ■ N ■ O ■ W ■ N ■ A ■ O ■
V E N D E U S E ■ D A M A G E
■ B ■ E ■ C ■ D ■ I ■ ■ ■ N ■
F O U R T H ■ I N A C T I O N
■ K ■ C ■ D ■ S ■ ■ ■ E ■ M ■
■ ■ A P O T H E C A R I E S ■
■ B ■ N ■ W ■ ■ ■ A ■ R ■ N ■
D R I V I N G F O R C E ■ ■ ■
■ E ■ A ■ ■ ■ A ■ D ■ S ■ P ■
P A S S O V E R ■ S E T T E R
■ T ■ ■ ■ E ■ E ■ H ■ R ■ S ■
S H O W E R ■ A R A B I S T S
■ E ■ A ■ N ■ S ■ R ■ A ■ E ■
F R A G M E N T ■ P A L T R Y
```

SOLUTIONS

61

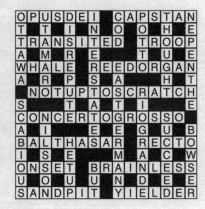

62

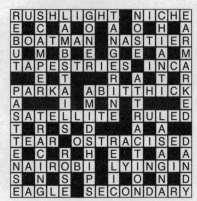

63

64

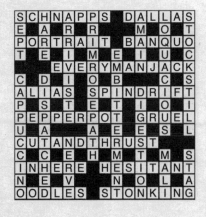

65

SITED EXCISEMAN
CLEOPATRA CONGO
EMPLOY EDENTATE
CHATELAINE WEEP
WATT DETACHMENT
GREENMAN PONCHO
LATHE DUBLINERS
DECADENCE REPLY

66

DESSERTS TWELVE
SUITEDANDBOOTED
GLOBULE NEWYEAR
UNDERSEA OREAD
PARIS THANATOS
CLAMOUR HALCYON
BACKTOSQUAREONE
RETORT STRESSED

67

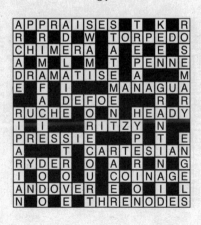

68

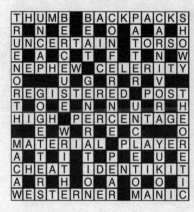

SOLUTIONS

69

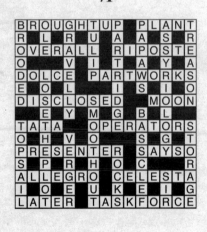

```
H A R D B A C K S   O R D E R
O   A   E   E   O   N   O   O
R I G H T O N   L E T I N T O
U   W   E   T   A   J   S
S T E R N   R E C A P T U R E
E   O   E   O       A   V
B E D   I N S E N T I E N C E
A   R   T   C   N       L
T R A V E L A G E N T   C U T
H   B   G   N   R   H
C L A S S I E S T   I R I S H
H   L   U   R   G   M   A
A D O R N E D   A C A D E M Y
P   N   U   U   T   N   R   D
S W E E P   O V E R T R A I N
```

70

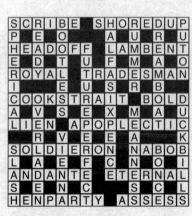

```
T R E A S U R E   F R A P P E
E   G   N   L   I   N   O
S P E E D M E R C H A N T
E   N   E   C   T   T
C R A T E R   T W I T C H E R
V   O       R   O   R
L E P R E C H A U N   M A Y O
A   O       A   P
E A R N   M A R B L E A R C H
P   G   E   E   R   O
C O V E N A N T   T I T I A N
S   G   R   O   M   S
T O O K A B A C K S E A T
L   W   I   C   E   N   E
B E R L I N   T I N C T U R E
```

71

```
B R O U G H T U P   P L A N T
R   L   R   U   A   A   S   R
O V E R A L L   R I P O S T E
O   V   I   T   A   Y   A
D O L C E   P A R T W O R K S
E   O   L   I   S   I   O
D I S C L O S E D   M O O N
E   Y   M   G   B   L
T A T A   O P E R A T O R S
O   H   V   O   S   G   T
P R E S E N T E R   S A Y S O
S   P   R   H   O   C   R
A L L E G R O   C E L E S T A
I   O   E   U   K   E   I   G
L A T E R   T A S K F O R C E
```

72

```
S C R I B E   S H O R E D U P
P   E   O   A   U   R   U
H E A D O F F   L A M B E N T
E   D   T   U   F   M   A   O
R O Y A L   T R A D E S M A N
I   E   U   S   R   B
C O O K S T R A I T   B O L D
A   V   S   E   X   M   A   U
L I E N   A P O P L E C T I C
R   V   E   E   A   K
S O L D I E R O N   N A B O B
L   A   E   F   C   N   O   I
A N D A N T E   E T E R N A L
S   E   N   C   S   C   L
H E N P A R T Y   A S S E S S
```

73

V	I	V	A	C	I	T	Y		C	A	N	N	A	E
E		I		H		W		S		E		L		L
N	I	T		U	N	I	N	H	A	B	I	T	E	D
I		R		C		S		E		O		B		O
C	R	I	C	K	E	T	B	A	T		F	A	I	R
E		O		S		T		D		I		L		A
	C	L	U	T	C	H		R	A	N	K	L	E	D
H			E		E		E		E		D			O
O	U	T	B	A	C	K		S	T	I	F	L	E	
T		H		K		N		T		A		E		B
W	A	R	D		M	I	C	R	O	N	E	S	I	A
I		O		B		F		A		C		O		N
R	A	W	M	A	T	E	R	I	A	L		T	O	G
E		I		L			N		U		H			O
D	U	N	L	I	N		S	T	U	B	B	O	R	N

74

D	O	W	N	R	I	G	H	T		S	H	R	E	W
E		I		A		A		R		P		O		I
M	O	T	E	T		R	E	A	L	I	S	T	I	C
I		H		A		D		N		E			K	
T	A	K	E	F	R	E	N	C	H	L	E	A	V	E
		N		I	N		E		E	N	D			
S	P	O	R	A	D	I	C		O	R	A	C	L	E
N		B			A		C			H			S	
A	B	S	E	I	L		R	O	O	D	L	O	F	T
R		O		N		W		M		O		R		
E	R	N	E	S	T	H	E	M	I	N	G	W	A	Y
D			P		E		U		E		O		E	
R	E	P	R	E	S	E	N	T		G	E	M	M	A
U		A		C		L		E		A			E	T
M	O	N	E	T		S	I	D	E	L	I	N	E	S

75

R	E	P	A	C	K		A	C	C	O	U	T	R	E
E		I		L		R		A		X		O		X
I	N	T	H	E	S	O	U	P		L	A	P	U	P
N		F		A		C		I		I		S		A
B	E	A	T	N	I	K		T	Y	P	H	O	O	N
A		L		R		Y		A		I		D		D
C	E	L	L	O		M	O	L	E	C	U	L	E	
K			O		O		O		O		O			T
	P	L	U	M	D	U	F	F		C	O	P	R	A
A		I		N		F		H		H		P		P
F	L	E	A	P	I	T		E	P	I	T	O	M	E
I		D		I		A		N		N		N		S
E	P	O	D	E		I	N	C	R	E	M	E	N	T
L		W		C		N		E		A		I		R
D	A	N	S	E	U	S	E		F	L	U	N	K	Y

76

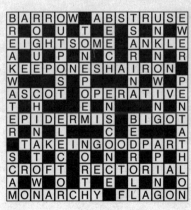

B	A	R	R	O	W		A	B	S	T	R	U	S	E
R		O		U		T		E		S		N		W
E	I	G	H	T	S	O	M	E		A	N	K	L	E
A		U		P		N		C		R		N		R
K	E	E	P	O	N	E	S	H	A	I	R	O	N	
W			S		P			N		W		W		P
A	S	C	O	T		O	P	E	R	A	T	I	V	E
T		H		E		N		N			N		N	
E	P	I	D	E	R	M	I	S		B	I	G	O	T
R		N		L		C		E			C		A	
	T	A	K	E	I	N	G	O	O	D	P	A	R	T
S		T		C		O		N		R		P		H
C	R	O	F	T		R	E	C	T	O	R	I	A	L
A		W		O		T		E		L			N	O
M	O	N	A	R	C	H	Y		F	L	A	G	O	N

SOLUTIONS

77

```
F R E T L E S S   S H A D O W
O O   A   O   R   O   R     R
R U N A T E M P E R A T U R E
M     E   M   S   X   M     A
U N F E T T E R E D   S M U T
L   O   A     M   A   A     H
A P R I C O T   B R I O C H E
    G   K   U   L   D     H
S T E L L A R   E L E G I A C
I   T   E M     D   N   A
N U M B   D E N O U E M E N T
E     E   A   R   G   C     A
W I N D C H I L L F A C T O R
E   O   C     E   M   O     R
D I T H E R   T R I P T Y C H
```

78

```
B O L L A R D   P E R I D O T
O   E   L   R   H   E   R   I
M A G N I F I C O   W H A N G
B   A   B   B   O   R   U   E
    T H I M B L E R I G G E R
S   E       L   Y   T   H   S
C H E R O K E E   S T I T C H
A   V   R   C   E         A
R E E F E R   T E E N A G E R
E   W   R   E   N     O   K
D R E S S E D T O K I L L
Y   L   I   I   T   N   I   L
C L A N G   S T A G E N A M E
A   M   H   O   P   R   T   F
T I B E T A N   H A T C H E T
```

79

```
T E S T A M E N T   T O P I C
R   I   T   P   A U   E   R
A R G O T   I M B A L A N C E
N   M   E   T   L   L   T   O
S T A U N C H   E Y E B A L L
M     U   E   A     G     E
  I N F R A S T R U C T U R E
T   E   T       R   A   K
  E L D E R S T A T E S M A N
A   O     H   C   N     O
F I N A G L E   C O C K P I T
R   I   R   R   U   H   O W
E C O N O M I C S   A D D L E
S   U   P   F   E   N   I   E
H A S T E   F I R S T H A N D
```

80

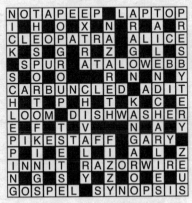

```
N O T A P E E P   L A P T O P
I   H   O   X   N   R   A   R
C L E O P A T R A   A L I C E
K   S   G   R   Z   G   L   S
  S P U R   A T A L O W E B B
S   O   O       R   N   N   Y
C A R B U N C L E D   A D I T
H   T   P   H   T   K   C   E
L O O M   D I S H W A S H E R
E   F   T   V       N   A   Y
P I K E S T A F F   G A R Y
P   I   E   L   I   A   L   Z
I N N I T   R A Z O R W I R E
N   G   S   Y   Z   O   E   U
G O S P E L   S Y N O P S I S
```

Explore more of the range from
THE ⚜ TIMES

Available from all good booksellers.

Follow us 🐦 @collinsdict

Join us 📘 'CollinsDictionary.com'